Asterian Astrology is revolutionary and will change the way we view Astrology forever.
Shri Ananda Das

Jade Luna has been amazing in assisting me in my career and my personal life.
Courteney Cox

I love Jade Luna's readings. He is the most pinpoint accurate astrologer out there. His system and guidance have been invaluable.
Rashida Jones

Jade Luna's wisdom and knowledge are matched perfectly with his heart and compassion. I am deeply grateful for his astrological guidance on my path.
Sheryl Lee

Jade Luna's system of astrology and his readings were extremely beneficial for me, giving me great insight and guidance.
Drena De Niro

Jade Luna's insight and understanding of the truth of astrology is outstanding. It has served me and stands to serve us all.
Regina Hall

From the moment we started, I knew I was in the presence of a studied and experienced reader whose depth of knowledge and experience in the field surpassed many clairvoyants. Jade Luna has an insightful gift of interpretation based on an original science that is irrefutable. He told me things my heart was quietly protecting, changed my regrets into benefits, and helped me release that which no longer served me. There is much to share about Jade Luna's readings, suffice it to say, I left with a peace I have not had in years. Thank you Jade for helping me value the journey.
Angela Gibbs

Jade Luna is a masterful Astrologer.
Terence Trent D'Arby

Asterian Astrology is a gem 2,300 years in the making.
Franl Lanz

I have found Jade Luna's talents to be extremely helpful and supportive to me staying on track in my life and achieving my personal goals.
Maxine Lapiduss

I have seen how transformative Jade Luna's teachings can be. For years, he has been my personal guide providing me with invaluable tools for my practice, work and life while helping me to access deeper spiritual dimensions. Jade is a powerful astrologer and mystic, who has a profound gift for making spirituality accessible in modern life today.
Bija Bennett

Jade Luna's astrological readings and revitalization of ancient Greek mysticism are amazing! I have gotten so much clarity from both aspects of Jade's work. And both have been instrumental in my continued growth in all aspects of my life.
Sharmila Devar

Jade Sol Luna INC Publishing

LUNA

Copyright.JadeLuna@AsterianAstrology
www.asterianastrology.com

We dedicate this book to those who desire to seek consciousness over commercialism.

Contents

Forward by Sharmila Devar   **Page 4**

Intro by Jade Luna   Page 7

The 27 Stars of Asterian Astrology   Page 9

Dioscuri **Page 10**
Hades **Page 15**
Vesta   **Page 20**
Pasiphae   **Page 25**
Prometheus **Page 30**
Typhon   **Page 35**
Artemis **Page 40**
Zeus   **Page 45**
Hydra **Page 50**
Persephone   **Page 55**
Bacchus   **Page 60**
Hymenaeus   **Page 65**
Sol   **Page 70**
Vulcan   **Page 75**
Favonius   **Page 80**
Dinus   **Page 85**
Urania   **Page 90**
Parca   **Page 95**
Hecate   **Page 100**
Ceto   **Page 105**
Natura   **Page 110**
Apollo   **Page 115**
Muses   **Page 120**
Aegeon   **Page 125**
Chimera   **Page 130**
Phorcus   **Page 136**
Hermaia   **Page 142**

Asterian Astrology and the 12 Sun signs   Page 147

Rahu and Ketu (Head and Body of Medusa) Page 160

Axial Precession   Page 166

Glossary 172

Forword
by Sharmila Devar

I first met Jade Luna in September of 2010. In the six months prior to our meeting, dramatic career and personal events brought tremendous upheaval to my life. My status quo, safe but ultimately unfulfilling, was being challenged by the universe and I was freaking out. (Thanks to Jade, I've since learned that chaos and reversals will be a constant in my life – so I'd better get used to them.) I needed help to find my bearings so I could maneuver the unknown reality of my "new" life.

So, when I scheduled my appointment with him, I figured I had nothing to lose. At worst, my visit would make a funny story to tell my friends over cocktails. However, Jade told me things about myself that I knew to be accurate on a subconscious level. That day, it became clear to me that fate or destiny or whatever you want to call it wanted me to use his knowledge to bring my shadows into the light. Interestingly, Jade gave his 27-sign system Greco/Roman mythological identifiers, yet his was a system based on Indian (Jyotish) astrology. This had personal relevance for me.

You see, I was born in the United States to Indian immigrant parents who sacrificed a lot to give my brother and me every opportunity to succeed. But we lived in a small town in the Midwest with very little culture outside of middle class, WASP life. I felt so different from my parents, though I loved them deeply. My favorite movies were American, preferably from the Golden Age of Hollywood. I definitely wasn't the poster child for my Midwestern Indian community.

Yet, the small town white Americans in my neighborhood and school could only see me as Indian. It was tough being different, and I grew up resenting being Indian. However, there was a significant side of me that loved being Indian. Because of it, I had had the opportunity to see the world at a young age. But being an outsider from both worlds created a chasm in my soul. I brought that conflict, kicking and screaming, into my adult life and into my first experience with Asterian Astrology.

When Jade explained that this system blended Indian astrology with Greek mythology (due to the influence of Alexander the Great), he had no clue that he had tapped into my soul's great conflict. But I was given a gift that day.

Significantly, in this initial session I learned that I was not an Aries – as I always had been told – but was ruled by a star in Pisces called Phorcus.

This was a relief, because Aries never quite fit me. I was a very shy and sensitive child, artistically-inclined and compassionate to a fault. Mostly, my time was spent with animals, or in my books and mind concocting fantasies, not a competitive, trailblazing Aries at all.

It is amazing how well the Asterian Astrology description of Pisces and Phorcus fit me. I have since learned that Phorcus is a mutable sign, explaining my chameleon-like tendencies – as an actress and in life. But, like life itself, there is another side to this astrological coin. As the Earth is affected by the cycles of the moon, so am I by my moon: Bacchus in the sign of Leo.

Like the Energizer Bunny, the bearers of Bacchus energy can just keep going and going. There are so many places to visit, people to meet, things to do! Also, like the lion who rules Leo, I feel it is my duty to protect those who are less fortunate, and I found a love of working with underprivileged children. Conversely, those of us ruled by Bacchus can be terribly vicious, punishing ourselves and others who don't live up to our own high expectations. So, watch out if you reach my threshold of disappointment!

Asterian Astrology also encourages exploration of the shadow side, uncovering the fear-based parts of my nature that keep me from reaching my full potential. This is so valuable. I even got tattoos of my Sun/Moon and Shadow Sun/Moon on my feet – as a constant reminder to walk steadily in this life as Sharmila Devar.

That is the goal, isn't it? Acceptance. Struggling against our basic nature is such a waste of energy. It is much more powerful and positive to accept it, learn from it and then move forward. I believe that the information in this book will show you the first steps you can take to accept yourself, in all your flawed glory.

I hope you enjoy the discovery as much as I have. Welcome to the adventure. You are in for a real treat!

Sharmila Devar
November, 2013

Hailing from a small suburb outside of Indianapolis, Indiana, Sharmila Devar is a classically trained actress who has performed on stages all over the United States. Favorite productions include AGAMEMNON, MEDEA, A MIDSUMMER NIGHT'S DREAM, OUR TOWN, CABARET, etc. at theatres such as South Coast Repertory (Costa Mesa, CA), Exit Theater (SF), East West Players (LA) and the prestigious Steppenwolf Theatre in Chicago, Illinois. Now based in Los Angeles, Ms. Devar has worked in several indie films including FEEL BETTER FAST and SHADES OF RAY. Most recently, she starred as a pregnant woman conflicted about motherhood in the dark comedy HAPPY AND YOU KNOW IT, written and directed by Deepti Gupta. Best known for her work on American television, she has guest starred on THE MENTALIST, JOEY, MONK, HOUSE, PRIVATE PRACTICE, ARRESTED DEVELOPMENT, and as Lata for 20 episodes of NBC's groundbreaking comedy, OUTSOURCED. Ms. Devar is currently enjoying her popularity as Lauren Wellman, President Grant's secretary on ABC's hit show SCANDAL. In her free time, she partakes in many hobbies, including volunteering for 826LA, yoga, rescuing neighborhood cats while gardening, gourmet cooking (and eating), and learning to play the acoustic guitar.

Introduction

By Jade Luna

The Earth wobbles; it does not have an even rotation. The system of Astrology that we use in the West does not follow the wobble of the Earth's axis, making all astrology off by 23 degrees. Regarding this, Western Astrologers say, "We do not follow the stars, we follow the seasons."

I say, "The seasons are different on this planet. We can not apply Northern hemisphere seasons to the whole globe and call that Astrology. The seasons in Australia are the exact opposite of the Northern hemisphere's, yet they use the same system! Also, Astrology means science of the stars, not science of the seasons.

They say, "We follow the Astrology system of the Babylonians." No, they do not! The Babylonians followed the Precession of the Equinoxes. All ancient cultures did. There is not a shred of evidence supporting a seasonal system in any ancient writings. All ancient cultures made their observations by looking up into the sky and observing the planets moving through the constellations.

I have also heard Western Astrologers state that the Zodiac is symbolic and the measurements are not important. This is the most deplorable belief, because it is a direct insult to our Astrologer ancestors, such as the Sumerians, Babylonians, and the Egyptians. They all erected planetariums and observatories just to calculate the position of the constellations, and the planets moving through them, as perfectly as possible.

Some say to me, "Well, you are an Eastern Astrologer, not a Western one." THAT IS FALSE. Alexander the Great was responsible for spreading the Egyptian system of Astrology to the East during his conquest. India and Tibet are the only places on earth that use the original Egyptian/Greco system of astrology that we call Eastern Astrology.

So what happened?

Around nineteen hundred years ago, something happened that had not happened in 26,000 years. The Zodiac aligned perfectly with the 12 month calendar which, in ancient times, was called "the Tropical Year." The most famous Astrologer of this time, Ptolemy, called the Zodiac the "Tropical Zodiac" due to this rare alignment. This alignment would last for only 72 years. In these 72 years, Rome created anti-divination laws, making Astrology illegal. So, Astrology was never able to evolve in the West, as it did in Eastern cultures. When you refer to Western Astrology, you are referring to a "Tropical Zodiac" that has not existed for 1900 years. Eastern cultures use the proper Zodiac. It is time that we do so as well.

Now you might ask, "Why do I feel like my Western sign?" The reason that you feel like the wrong sign is because you have been reading and relating to it your entire life. It is called the power of suggestion, but it is not who you are; and it is not your role in the universe.

The 27 Stars of Asterian Astrology

If you are born on a cusp (day that the sun shifts signs), contact an Asterian Astrologer to get your sign. The dates listed under the Star name are for 1946 to 2017. Also located under the Star name are the degrees. If you know your sidereal degrees, you can find your Moon and Rising traits here as well.

Dioscuri

April 13th – April 26th

00.00 degrees to 13.20 Aries

Animal – Horse

Planet - Ketu

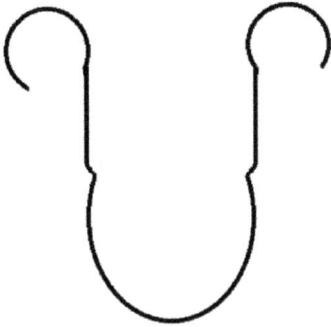

If you were born under this star, you're probably not surprised to find that it's the first one of the astrological year. You've known this all your life, haven't you? You feel a natural desire to lead, to be first, to forge into new areas. Fearless and curious (some might call it foolhardy, but what do they know?), Dioscuri people love to start things and break new ground. What's more, you seem to be able to convince others that you know what you're doing, no matter how hopeless things might look on the surface.

Why is that? Because those born under Dioscuri are seen as the fix-it folks, intelligent and levelheaded. You are the one that gets asked how to work something out, how to solve a problem, or to give sage advice on something particularly prickly. And you respond, don't you? Even if you don't have a specific solution. After all, deep down inside you know that it's your mission to be of service, to guide lost souls to a better day.

It's natural that others see you this way, too. The gods of this sign, the Dioscuri, were traditionally known for their kindness to humans. Horsemen, they were said to ride to the rescue and to protect those who asked for their help. As a person born under Dioscuri, you have these qualities. This is what you are all about.

In mythology, the Dioscuri were brothers who shared a mother, but different fathers. One was born of a mortal, but the other was a son of Zeus, the king of the gods. So between them they understood both the common and the sublime. They eventually became guardians in the afterlife, each spending time in Heaven and in Hades. They were honored by becoming the twin stars of Gemini, Castor and Pollux, even though Dioscuri is the first star in Aries as well, wholly contained within that Sun sign..

The animal for your sign is the horse, and the symbol for the sign is the horse's head, with good reason. The horse has been the helpmate of humans for thousands of years. Enlisted to assist people travel, plow their fields, perform for their amusement, even carry them into battle, the horse has a revered place in many cultures. This is why others tend to look to you for assistance.

While this is all well and good, you must be mindful of the dark side. Look at the natural environment of the horse. It is a creature that longs to be free, to run wild in nature. However, the frequent home for a horse is a stable, a place of confinement. Helping has a cost, and it is a cost that the Dioscuri must always keep in mind.

It can happen that helping others becomes a burden. Horses bear their riders and pull their plows, but without a rest or some freedom, they can't remain healthy. And don't try to get away with telling yourself that you can do it all, all the time. That typical, stubborn streak only causes trouble for the children of the horse lords.

In other words, when someone wants to take a ride, there are times when you'll have to tell them that they need to walk instead. This isn't being selfish; it's taking care of yourself, so you can help others more fully. A self-neglecting Dioscuri doesn't do anyone any good.

Those born under this star are often respected and sought after. That's because your rep is one of honesty, trustworthiness, and optimism. You've got personal magnetism to burn, and can enjoy "horsing around" quite a bit. But what most people don't see is your contemplative side. The myth of the Dioscuri shows why you have these two sides.

As someone born under Dioscuri, you have an inherent ability to see both the Light and the Dark, and you have an intuitive understanding that both exist in everything. This ability is aided by your star being ruled by the South Node of the Moon (also called Cauda Draconis, the Dragon's Tail, or Ketu, its Hindu name). The South Node brings to those born under it strong intuitive abilities and an interest in the occult or unconventional. You therefore know that it is important to blend Light and Dark in looking at any problem. This is why you are so good at seeing the depths of difficulties and coming up with the best solution.

Being a child of this star, you have a quick intellect (a trait you share with those born under the sun sign of Gemini), and this will stay with you all of your days. By the way, be prepared for lots of days, as the Dioscuri tend to enjoy long life. The quickness you possess also characterizes so much about you. Have people said that you move too fast? Answer too quickly, dare we say impulsively? Have a lead foot while driving? All these are part of your Dioscuri legacy, one that comes naturally from your sign being entirely in the astrological Sun sign of Aries, ruled by Mars. Now, this can make you a formidable opponent in sports, business, or battle, for sure. You want to get in there and mix it up – and fast. But let's pull back on the reins a little bit. Remember that you have the ability to see both sides of an issue, and deeply at that. Certainty and confidence are great; just make sure that you've looked at everything before you gallop in one direction or another. Speed does not always equal efficiency, Dioscuri.

Many times, you are the one who sets the way, and you are great at beginning enterprises, especially those born from your fertile intellect and imagination. Sticking with things, however, can be difficult. You are always looking for the next challenge, the next problem to solve. Learning patience and persistence are some of the lessons of this sign.

In relationships, those born under Dioscuri are seen as faithful and devoted. You know that you will go out of your way to assist and accommodate those you care for. But again, don't forget to take time for yourself. There is no selfishness here. You will be more present for others if you are aware of, and take care of, your own needs. Additionally, there are times when you will be so excited about your next project or idea that you become separated from your emotions. This can leave those you care for feeling neglected. Remember to continue to consider those close to you, even when your mind is running free as the wind.

Dioscuri individuals are also often great healers, as they can see the root of a problem and figure out an effective solution. So, look for satisfaction if you decide to enter the field of medicine, either mainstream or alternative. As a convincing communicator, you can also be a gifted salesperson of products and ideas. This strength allows you to bring others into seeing things your way. Used properly, it is a great boon; improperly, it can be used to take advantage of the unwary.

Since your opinion is sought after, it puts you in a position of power. With this position comes the responsibility to use that power wisely. You often lead the way and others will follow you, no matter the path. Beware of arrogance, however. Those born under Dioscuri can lead their followers to the greatest heights or the deepest depths. Just as a principled Dioscuri can be magnificent, an unprincipled one can be very inconsiderate, irresponsible, and downright cruel. Apply this talent for leadership with the respect and discernment it deserves.

Horses love to travel, and you are no different, whether that travel is in the physical, mental, or spiritual realms. You are a great dreamer, and much inspiration will come to you through your dreams. You also have a natural attraction for esoteric areas like astrology or other occult sciences.

To be able to travel, it is important for those born under Dioscuri to see to their health. Since you will probably live a long life, it is essential to be sure to stay healthy. Dioscuri profit well from techniques that prolong life and keep the mind sharp. Also, since you are always looking for a new project to start, any self-improvement program will yield positive results if you stick with it (although sticking with it can be a challenge for the Dioscuri). By the same token, engaging in practices that are unhealthful, such as the misuse of intoxicants, poor diet, and general inactivity are not doing you any favors at all. You are a thoroughbred, Dioscuri; don't turn yourself into a broken-down nag.

Dioscuri, you are a wonderful combination of the free and the devoted, the Light and the Dark, the leader and the helper, the brash and the considerate. A balanced blend of these qualities will bring you the greatest peace and happiness. Enjoy your free mind and your ability to help others. Be the example and the ready assistant. Optimistic and a leader – run, Dioscuri, run!

1804 – 1875 Dioscuri, April 11 - 24
1875 – 1946 Dioscuri, April 12 - 25
1946 – 2017 Dioscuri, April 13 - 26
2017 – 2088 Dioscuri, April 14 - 27
2088 – 2159 Dioscuri, April 15 - 28
2159 – 2230 Dioscuri, April 16 - 29

Hades

April 27th – May 10th

13.20 degrees to 26.40 Aries

Animal – Elephant

Planet - Venus

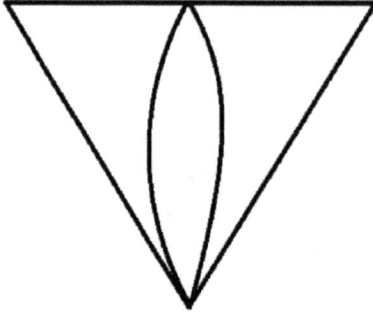

Well, Hades, let's not beat around the bush. Everybody knows that you love getting right to the point. So, here it is: You can handle the heavy stuff. In fact, you welcome it. You know, stuff like death and the meaning of life. But you come by it honestly, that's for sure. After all, the god of your sign is none other than the god of the underworld, and he's not one that anybody associates with superficiality.

How did Hades wind up with the underworld as his realm? The story goes that he and his brothers, Zeus and Poseidon, drew lots to see who would get to be the boss of what. Hades wound up with the underworld, and, by all accounts was a tad bitter about it. That resentment he felt can tinge your mood as well. But it's not because you're wallowing in spilt milk. Not usually, anyway. Most often, your dissatisfaction shows up when others don't see your point; and someone born under Hades always has a point.

To say that you are opinionated would be, shall we say, accurate. But it's not like you're spouting off, or shooting from the hip with some half-formed idea. That's not your style. Those under the influence of Hades are thinkers, and deep thinkers to boot. Any opinions you have come from long periods of thought and hard-won experience. And hard-won it often is, as those born under this star are commonly the tough luck ones, mirroring their god's outcome in the whole, brotherly "let's draw lots" affair.

Life for a Hades is often strewn with obstacles and setbacks, but you are the better for it. Hades demands that you face and overcome fear, especially fear of death, the ultimate fear for many. Now, there are some born under Hades who are unable or unwilling to confront fear. These folks tend to run in the other direction, becoming preoccupied with "sweetness and light," and denying the darkness entirely. To do this, however, would betray your life purpose. The tried and true Hades will wade right in, unafraid. They become the model for direct confrontation with the ultimate mystery. They wear the scars of their adventures with pride.

The investigation of death and dying is a core issue for those born of Hades. It can be accomplished in a number of ways, such as through science, philosophy, or art. But it needs to be approached in some fashion in order to be true to your nature. You know this inherently. The form that the investigation takes is up to you, and this leads to the lessons for those born under this star.

There are a couple of big lessons for all Hades. First, they must cultivate their creative side. Even though Hades is contained entirely within Mars-ruled Aries, this particular star is ruled by Venus, so it has a strong Venusian influence. Venus demands beauty and creativity. How to reconcile this? Hades must find a constructive way to express the emotions that they experience during their challenging times. The visual arts, music, writing – whatever is their preference.

This is absolutely essential because carrying and confronting the darkness is hard, demanding work. Without a creative outlet, not only do the experiences take their psychological toll on a Hades, but others will never truly feel the depth of the Hades experience. Communicating this depth is a Hades responsibility, and creative expression is the best way of allowing others into the depths. It's much better than being harangued by an inspired, opinionated Hades.

Believe it or not, child of Hades, this can be an unpleasant experience for those not born under the influence of the lord of the underworld.

Of course, this tendency to see and experience the darkness does not make those born under Hades evil or morose. In fact, they can be quite intelligent and kind at heart. However, Hades, you tend to be serious. Very. Serious. This tendency can make you a real drag to be around, and, frankly, you might even become fairly off-putting sometimes. But this brings up the second great lesson for those of Hades birth: Lighten up! However, this is something that does not come naturally for those of this star. Hades himself had a tough time with this one, and even his wife Persephone needed big chunks of time away from him. So, yeah, this will be a big challenge for the children of the lord of the underworld.

But there's hope. In the song entitled "Anthem," Leonard Cohen wrote, "There is a crack, a crack, in everything; that's how the light gets in." Finding the crack that lets in the light is a prime task for a Hades. You must find out how the light gets in, and follow it out. This is the way to overcome an obsession with the dark, and it often shows the way to the creative outlet so important for your own well-being. This is the way to peace for you, Hades.

In relationships, those born of Hades need to realize that they have an intensity not usually matched by those born of other stars. As such, it is important for them to lighten up (oh, there's that lesson again) and enjoy the other for who they are. Compromise is important, and even though your opinions may be strong, you have to make room for others, Hades. Allow enjoyment to enter whenever you can. Your creativity will lend an important energy to any relationship, so let the juices flow.

Careers that appeal to a Hades temperament include any that embrace investigation into the unknown, even unconventional subjects like UFOs! Given your strong creative flair, the arts in all their many forms would be rewarding. Also, let's face it, Hades, you love to argue and convince others of your point of view. Lawyer, professor, even politician – the vista is broad for someone born under Hades.

Children of Hades tend to live long lives. Since they are an intense breed, though, the ability to handle stress is paramount to their being able to live that long life healthily. To keep the effects of accumulated stress at bay, Hades must pursue a creative outlet. Keeping all that need to dive deep trapped within yourself is inviting disaster. Pursue whatever outlet you are called to, so that the high energy generated by your intense striving is effectively communicated and dissipated. By following your creative urge, you will be doing yourself and the rest of the world a great service.

Like death, sex is one of life's great mysteries. The symbol for this sign represents the grouping of three stars in Aries called the Buckle of Isis. This was seen as a portal between worlds by the ancients. Physically, this is represented by the vaginal opening, our portal between gestation and earthly life. Hades is quite comfortable exploring the sexual arena. Those of this star have an inherent feel for the great power of this force. Their fascination can take many forms, from being a champion for equality and the elevation of women, to falling prey to sexual addiction. Shining the light of exploration into the dark places while not being consumed by them. The task of the Hades life.

The animal associated with the star of Hades is the elephant. Regarded with much affection by people, the elephant is known for its generally peaceful ways, strong ability to form attachments, as well as its memory and intellectual prowess. This is much like the Hades individual. Often of a serious exterior, children of Hades have a strong intellect and are quite attached to their attitudes, ways of doing things, and those they hold dear.

When roused, however, an elephant is a fearsome creature, able to charge with such force that all other animals clear out of its way. This is Hades at its most resolute and determined, a formidable opponent in any situation. Unfortunately, this also leads many to see a Hades as dogmatic, unyielding, and stubborn. Ask a Hades, though, and they will tell you that is only because they are right, and you are wrong. Hmmm, maybe another area where you could lighten up a bit, Hades?

Those born of Hades carry a lesson for all of humanity. They show the world that great things can come from difficulty, and that adversity can be a source of prosperity. Through discipline and self-control, Hades shows the way to true accomplishment. Take that, Zeus and Poseidon!

1804 – 1875 Hades, April 25 – May 8
1875 – 1946 Hades, April 26 – May 9
1946 – 2017 Hades, April 27 – May 10
2017 – 2088 Hades, April 28 – May 11
2088 – 2159 Hades, April 29 – May 12
2159 – 2230 Hades, April 30 – May 13

Vesta

May 11th – May 23rd

26.40 degrees Aries to 10.00 Taurus

Animal – Ram

Planet - Sun

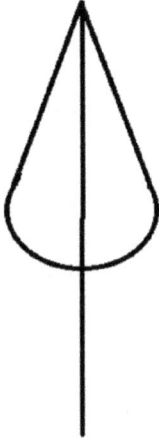

Vesta, you are a study in contrasts – but that's not intimidating to you at all. You actually enjoy it, as it is the natural state of your fiery spirit and insightful mind. You are very much at home in any situation that requires detailed investigation or one that presents a thorny intellectual challenge.

So, what's the smart thing to do if you need an accurate and careful assessment of a situation? Call a Vesta, of course. They glory in that kind of environment. It's just the sort of thing that allows Vesta to share its gifts. Nothing like a problem with twists and turns to get a Vesta interested. But it's not just in the intellectual sphere where Vestas show a knack. They're just as at home, well, at home.

Actually, this brings us to the first of the contrasts for which Vesta is so aptly known. Vesta (Hestia in Greek) was the goddess of the hearth, which was the center of the home, and the source of heat and food preparation in the ancient world. In other words, she was the goddess of security and sustenance in the personal abode. Yet, over time she also became the guardian of the state, as she watched over the fire of the home country. This gives Vestas the ability to keep an eye on their own homestead as well as on the larger affairs of the community. In other words, those born under this star are natural multi-taskers.

Moreover, the contrasts keep coming. You need look no farther than the mythology of this goddess in order to see it. Vesta, as Hestia, was the first born of the Titan named Kronos, who had a nasty habit of devouring his children. When this model for a poor father figure was finally dispatched by his young son Zeus, the previously devoured children sprang forth. Vesta, being the first eaten, was the last out of daddy's stomach. In so doing, she became the youngest of the re-born offspring. Both first and last. Those born under Vesta, therefore, can often see multiple perspectives.

Astrologically, this contrast viewpoint makes a lot of sense, too. You see, Vesta is one of the stars that crosses sun signs, in this case spanning late Aries and early Taurus. As someone born under Vesta, you are fortunate enough to have a bit of both of these powerful signs in your makeup. For instance, you certainly can be the hard-driving Aries, taking the lead and forging ahead. You can also be the more cautious Taurus, laying back and keeping your own counsel. This flexibility of character is something you should feel comfortable with. While others may find it a bit confusing, this won't seem all that strange to you. It's just that there are times when you will need the motivation of external factors to get you going. It's all in keeping with the Vesta way, going from smoldering embers to blazing fire.

On top of your mental prowess, you also have a spiritual side, Vesta. Metaphysically, fire is associated with the spirit, and sacrifices were traditionally burned so that the smoke and flame could carry the offerings to the gods. So again, Vesta-child, you present a seeming paradox. Spiritual on the one hand, while logical, even scientific, on the other. There is a great advantage here, giving you the ability to see a problem or question from multiple perspectives, from the practical to the philosophical and metaphysical.

Of course, you know that you have to watch your tongue, Vesta. There is a tendency to speak abruptly and sometimes harshly. It might even be said that you have a knack for blunt, unskillful language. And not without reason. Granted, you are quick and insightful. You can grasp things readily, and you have a need to speak your mind. But, not being one to suffer fools gladly, you can come across at times as rather harsh and critical. The result is that you use your sharp (spear tip) tongue to come up with caustic (fiery) comments. In other words, you can be a full-bore flamer sometimes! While you may be right, and you often are, diplomacy may be called for. Let the more sedate side of your psyche intervene when you are tempted to blaze away. It will pay dividends.

There is a great desire in you to achieve, which comes from the fiery side of your nature. You may find yourself jumping in, championing a social cause, for instance. Going after the deep truths and the greatest justice is what motivates you, Vesta. You see injustice and want to right it. You see suffering and want to alleviate it. This is the noblest part of your nature.

The earthy side of your star loves the home and children. It is a great desire of a Vesta to influence the next generation, to fill them with the right ethics and attitude, and to encourage positive, society affirming behaviors.

The dark side of Vesta, though, results from an imbalance in either of its two elemental influences of Fire and Earth. A Fire imbalance brings about a stubborn and aggressive disposition, not a pretty sight in someone who can be as driven as you. There can be problems in the social sphere, making for a combative, disagreeable person – even someone who has serial extra-marital affairs. Unbalanced Fire can also result in problems managing money, and Vesta can easily overspend or manage money poorly. An Earth imbalance can result in problems with motivation or poor dietary habits. In both cases, the elemental imbalances stem from a problem with managing desire. A major lesson for Vesta is coming to grips with the traps of misdirected desire. It is a problem that manifests in all forms of over-indulgence, including food, spending, sexual behavior, you name it. Bottom line? Just because you want it, Vesta, doesn't mean you should have it! Remember, the worst statement a Vesta can make is Oscar Wilde's famous, "I can resist anything except temptation."

In relationships, the balanced Vesta is devoted and loving. Defense of the hearth is a Vesta's pride, so providing for the home and the family is central to that Vesta need for achievement. It is important to be sure, however, to give the other person a fair chance at expressing their needs. You have strong opinions, Vesta-child, but others have theirs (and feelings, too). Caring parents, Vestas are protective and doting. They love to see their children succeed, and will do whatever they can to help that happen.

Various careers can be satisfying to someone born under this star. Any arena that allows for achievement and presents a challenge would be ideal. The law, engineering, cooking, or interior design are good examples. Working with charitable organizations will appeal to the Vesta sense of justice, and any career related to the home and its proper maintenance will give any Vesta a deeply fulfilled sense.

To remain healthy, those born of Vesta need to keep their desire nature under good control. Abuse of body or mind by giving in to unrestrained desire, while a problem for anyone, is especially bad for Vesta. Poor eating habits, lack of physical exercise, risky sexual behavior – all of these will give the Vesta particular problems. Those born under this star would do well to moderate their activity, and indulge in practices that bring gradual mastery to the desire nature. Leisure activities that are pleasing to the senses while also healing and revitalizing are best. Finally, try not to overextend yourself, Vesta. While you are talented, you have your limits.

The symbol for Vesta is a flame that resembles a spear tip. This is no accident. Your fondness for the home fire is a natural match for your determination to protect what is yours. You make no bones about how you feel, as your opinions are strongly held and defended with equal strength. After all, the animal for your sign is a ram. Blessed with an incisive and quick mind, Vestas are more than able to hold their own in arguments. However, be careful of times when your mental processes could trap you in over-thinking. This could lead to procrastination and inefficiency.

Bottom line? Reconciling contrasts is the task, Vesta. Flexible, yet disciplined. This balance will make it easy for you to keep the hearth fire burning brightly.

1804 – 1875 Vesta, May 09 - 21
1875 – 1946 Vesta, May 10 - 22
1946 – 2017 Vesta, May 11 - 23
2017 – 2088 Vesta, May 12 - 24
2088 – 2159 Vesta, May 13 - 25
2159 – 2230 Vesta, May 14 - 26

Pasiphae

May 24 - June 6
10.00 degrees to 23.20 Taurus

Animal – Snake

Planet - Moon

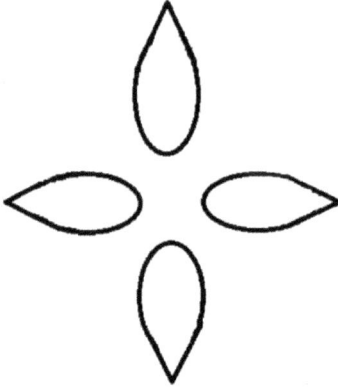

How can you feel bad if you were born under this star? You are one of the lucky ones! Pasiphae has endowed you with many gifts. You have an inborn charisma, and have an easy grace with the material world. Others are naturally attracted to you -- and you know it. Why wouldn't they be? You have a way with words, and your style is elegant. You have an affinity for the finer things, and you look fantastic surrounded by them. When the poet wrote, "She walks in beauty as the night, of cloudless climes and starry skies," he was talking about you.

Mythologically, Pasiphae was a child of the sun god Helios, and reflected his light just as the physical Moon does. She became a queen of Crete, but was cursed and her darkest qualities asserted themselves. She grew so obsessed with lust for the sacred bull (in Greek, Serapis – an earth god) that she mated with him and bore the Minotaur, a hybrid creature part man, part bull.

The metaphor of this story is a clear exposition of the traits of those born under Pasiphae. Sexuality and sensuality are definitely apparent, as well as the problem of over-identification with these currents. However, there is an indication of strong fertility and a natural affinity for the Earth (Taurus, the bull, is the fixed Earth sign). This is what gives you your green thumb, aiding in the creation and growth of everything you touch. Finally, the union with the bull god matches the position of Pasiphae in the sky, contained wholly within the solar sign of Taurus.

The Moon is often symbolized in mythology as a beautiful woman. She possesses an easy, seductive, sexual magnetism. As a child of Pasiphae, you also have this, in spades. You may find partners flocking to you, and your relationship skills keep the embers glowing. This ease that you possess gives you a desirable, down-to-earth quality that many will find irresistible. You are indeed a fortunate one.

All of this is no accident, as you are the favorite of the Moon herself. Of all of the 27 stars, the Moon has chosen yours as her natural abode. As a result, she has bestowed upon you all the mystery and subtle beauty of Luna, the Moon goddess. This lunar energy is one of the two great currents of existence. It signifies the soft, gentle, but irresistible power of the Moon. Mysterious, fascinating, and seductive. All these are the birthright of those born under this star.

The Pasiphae have an allure. More classy than flashy, they are comfortable with all things luxurious. Face it, Pasiphae, you can pull it off. You "wear it" in a way that shouts elegance. Your kind are the men and women who can carry off the latest styles as if those styles were created especially for them . . . and perhaps they were.

You are a sensual and sensitive creature, Pasiphae. You live in the world of the senses and are acutely aware of their impact on your mood. Because of this it is important to surround yourself with harmonious and pleasant stimuli. You crave this deeply, and strive to make the world a more beautiful place for everyone.

These natural abilities have a dark side, however. Pasiphae natives can be quite judgmental at times. Oh, yes, Pasiphae, you can be a snob.

With your natural grace and elegance, you can find it easy to look down your nose at those less fortunate. But be kind, favorite of the Moon. Not everyone can see with your discerning eye or your sensitive ear. Your job is to enlighten, not to denigrate. Your mission is to bring beauty to the world, making it a more harmonious place.

Unfortunately, you inspire envy as well as admiration. Face it, your detractors wish that they had your elegance and attractiveness. There's not much you can do about that, though. Uplift and inspire -- this is your best course of action. You already know how persuasive you can be. You are bright and clever, and your voice has a calming and convincing quality. Use it wisely, gently bringing others around to your perspective.

Marriage is important to the Pasiphae spirit, as it is another way to express creativity and growth. The raising of children feeds the desire to bring beauty into the world, and to instill the next generation with values that treasure the finest that life has to offer. Your relationship life is important to you, and you should be sure to find a partner that is supportive and faithful. You have many gifts to share in this realm, and you would be best served by sharing them with someone who could truly appreciate them, while giving you the freedom to express who you are at your core.

Professionally, Moon children shine in areas that encourage creativity, growth, and the development of beauty, like agriculture, writing, acting, and the arts. Those born under Pasiphae also love to have order in the world, and like to see and engage in proper behavior. (Some might call it conventional, but you know it is what keeps everything working as it should.) For Pasiphae, uncontrolled growth is like unrestrained urges. It is the road to chaos. Any endeavor that allows them to be an example of order and proper behavior is also appealing. Also, don't be loathe to travel or have a career that involves it. Pasiphae loves to see the world in all its beauty. Seeing and experiencing earthly beauty in all its forms nourishes your spirit and considerable lust for life.

There are other wonderful advantages to being one of those in close harmony with the Moon. For instance, your greatest path to health is to be in tune with cycles. The Moon has her regular cycle, which has a pervasive impact on people, as well as on the Earth itself. Regularity is the key. Don't be afraid of routines, Pasiphae. These are the anchors that allow your more experimental, experiential side to flourish. Eating regular, healthful meals, and engaging in regular exercise will maximize Pasiphae's tendency for long life. Be sure to pick foods and exercises that appeal to your own sense of rhythm and beauty. These are the things that will feel the best and bring optimal results. Beware, though, of excess self-indulgence and complacency. These tendencies are the road to ruin for you. They are truly the dark side of the Moon. Remember the myth!

When under stress, those with a Pasiphae heritage should take time to meditate on the beauty of nature, especially nature that has been ordered and beautified to the highest degree by the intervention of caring people. Visions of lush, wondrous gardens; the sights and sounds of fields of ripening grain; experiences of deep-felt love – all of these are nourishing to the Pasiphae spirit.

It's no surprise that the symbol for this sign is a four-petaled flower. Children of Pasiphae have a natural flare for cultivating and growing things, and they would find themselves happily placed in an orchard, on a farm, or in a garden. After all, the best way to plant things is by the Moon's phases, isn't it? Of course, many things can be cultivated, including relationships, businesses, finances, etc. Here is where you shine, Pasiphae. It's your ability to make things grow, and to make things beautiful. Take anything and invest it with your effort and appreciation of beauty. It will be the better for it. The animal that represents your sign is a snake, a creature associated with wisdom, but also with guile. The snake's flicking tongue takes in the world, as your acute senses do. But that tongue also symbolizes your cleverness. This is a creature that sheds its skin as it grows, and you will find yourself shifting perspectives and shedding old viewpoints as your sense of the world matures. Also, notice the easy, sinuous movements of a snake as it travels its environment. Your graceful movements are very much like this. The snake is an object of fascination and fear, just as you are an object of desire and envy. How you handle this immense personal power is up to you.

At the base of it all are your emotions. They are key, Pasiphae, since the Moon is closely linked to the emotional nature of humankind. Observe your feelings carefully to gauge your equilibrium and strive to keep your emotions moderate and mild. This is your road to great, inner peace.

Tethered to the Earth, spiritually linked to the lunar vibration, passionate and creative, Pasiphae offers a grand example of the joy of earthly existence. And that's no bull!

1804 – 1875 Pasiphae, May 22 – June 4
1875 – 1946 Pasiphae, May 23 – June 5
1946 – 2017 Pasiphae, May 24 – June 6
2017 – 2088 Pasiphae, May 25 – June 7
2088 – 2159 Pasiphae, May 26 – June 8
2159 – 2230 Pasiphae, May 27 – June 9

Prometheus

June 07 – June 20
23.20 degrees Taurus to 06.40 Gemini

Animal – Snake

Planet - Mars

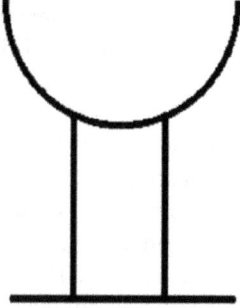

Prometheus, here's the difference between you and most other people. Most people will look in this book and read about their own sign, and possibly those of their loved ones. But not you. You, born under the star of Prometheus, will probably read every one of these descriptions. Why? Because you just have to know about it all. It's part and parcel of who you are.

Prometheus, you are a seeker, plain and simple. Striving is in your blood. The desire to discover, to find out, is an essential part of who you are. You live by the immortal words of Robert Browning, "A man's reach should exceed his grasp – or what's a heaven for?" Given the god of this star, it's no surprise at all. Prometheus was the adventurer of the Titans in ancient mythology. He was also a good friend – some might even say a protector – of humanity. He saw suffering creatures and sought to relieve their pain. He gave humankind the great gift of fire. Sadly, he paid dearly for it. He was chained to a mountain side by the gods and had his liver eaten on a daily basis by an eagle. That's right, every blessed day. By an eagle. But Prometheus must have had the fastest regenerating organs ever known, because his liver grew back every night, only to have it eaten again the next day. This went on for ages, until he was released by Hercules.

Even knowing that he would probably suffer for his gift to humanity didn't stop him, just as you won't be deterred in the pursuit of knowledge, come what may. The children of Prometheus are the life-long students of the zodiac. Thirst for knowing is at their core. They have contributed much to the evolution of knowledge and don't show any sign of slowing down.

It's just so much fun isn't it, Prometheus? It's almost as if the pursuit is the important thing, even more than the goal sometimes. Few can hold this endless pursuit against you, either. You're just so darn affable. You're the good-natured seeker, always off on an adventure of the mind or body. Yes, you pursue physical quests as well. The offspring of Prometheus are often interested in sports, and test themselves on the playing field with gusto.

There's no doubt that this is an enjoyable star to be born under. The children of Prometheus are most often of a lighthearted nature, and have a life filled with curiosity. What's more, they are just as comfortable in an office as in a nature preserve. This is due to the position of this star in the zodiac, spanning the last part of Taurus and the first part of Gemini. Your Taurean nature, Prometheus, lends you a love of art, beauty, and the finer things – all things of a Venusian bent. Your easy-going style is also a gift from the sign of the bull. Your intellectual curiosity, quick wit, and clever approach to problems all come from Gemini and fast-thinking Mercury. The combination gives you the advantage of being nosey without being obnoxious. Most people are amused by you and will enjoy hearing about your latest discoveries and adventures. This is good, because you love to talk and are a gifted storyteller, child of the Fire-Bringer.

There are some dark aspects to Prometheus, however, and these are shown in the traditional dark sides of the two sun signs that compose this star. The negative expression of Taurus results in laziness and self-indulgence. This is extremely damaging to your desire to strive,

Prometheus, and can only lead to dissatisfaction and self-criticism, as your Gemini mind gets into the act. Speaking of which, your busy mind can also get caught in a loop, leading to obsessive thinking – mentally spinning your wheels. This is like Prometheus getting his liver eaten day after day. You can save yourself from this problem by calling on the strength of Hercules; that is, by drawing on your inner desire to strive and engage in the pursuit of knowledge and understanding. This will serve to free you from the negative expressions of your star. And how much better you will feel when you do this! No child of Prometheus likes to be tied down or to be mired in heavy situations. Express your freedom and all will be well. Let your light-hearted nature shine through!

Relationships with a Prometheus individual can be challenging, however. This tendency to focus on the pursuit rather than the goal can be vexing for anyone in such a relationship. There is a definite drive in the Prometheans not to settle down, or to be stable with one thing. Unless this restlessness can be channeled, frustration will definitely arise in most cases. To be successful in relationships, Prometheus must learn to balance the thrill of the quest with the stability of achieving the goal. Fortunately, it is in your nature to do so, Prometheus. You have a strong Taurean undercurrent; and Taurus is stable and solid. With some effort, you can still let your Gemini mind out to play while keeping it anchored with earthy Taurus.

Another potential stumbling block for Prometheus in relationships is a tendency to have a great interest in many potential mates. Your questing urge comes to the fore here too, as it does in so many areas. The fact that you project a gentle, graceful aura will attract attention, of course. Adding to your attraction is the fact that you can turn a clever phrase and enchant many with your gift of gab.

Obviously, keeping yourself in a stable relationship can be challenging if the lure of another pursuit is never far from your mind. Look but don't touch, Prometheus, if you are in a stable relationship of your liking. Otherwise, constantly playing the field will be the story of your love life.

Clever by nature, the Prometheans are at home in careers that require an inquisitive mind and a dogged determination to discover. Research occupations tend to be very satisfying for those born under this star. This can encompass everything from being an author of travel articles to being a librarian. Also, Prometheus is comfortable both in the lab and in the field, as long as there are discoveries to be made and learning to be done. For you, there is no greater joy than learning something new, finding out, discovering. And, to be honest, who cares if it's immediately useful or applicable, Prometheus? Finding things out is the great pleasure. Of course, if whatever is discovered can be applied to something practical, so much the better, but it's OK by Prometheus in any case. After all, when is knowledge not cool?

The health of those born under Prometheus is assured by careful attention to diet. Avoid anything that slows down your digestion. This will keep constipation, both physical and mental, at bay. Also, since Taurus and Gemini rule the throat, shoulders, and arms, be careful of strain to those areas. Protect yourself from colds and sore throats by covering up whenever it is appropriate. Additionally, you tend to have a nervous, restless streak. Therefore, a calm spirit is a must. What is best for your spirit, Prometheus, is to keep occupied with intellectual pursuits and those things which bring you the greatest sense of fulfillment. Meditation will also calm the mind in anxious times. Be sure not to waste your resources on frivolous things – well, at least not very often. You will wind up feeling unsatisfied, and can slip into negative states of mind as a result.

The symbol of this sign is a blending of the signs of Taurus and Gemini, with the twins supporting the horns of the bull. This symbol can also be seen as a cup, collecting the nectar of knowledge. Endeavor to keep the cup full at all times, so you can freely dispense the results of your quest to those around you.

The animal associated with the sign of Prometheus is the snake. In this case, it is not a vicious or poisonous reptile, but a gentle, harmless one. This is the snake that is the symbol of acquired wisdom, able to squirm into the smallest of places in the name of finding it all out. As you continue to develop, Prometheus, you will find yourself shedding your old skin, just like the snake. Growing in knowledge and wisdom, you will fulfill your greatest need.

Well balanced children of Prometheus are a joy to all who encounter them. Face it; yours is an enviable sign, Prometheus. You are imaginative, interesting, and well liked. With your active mind, you are almost never bored, and always ready to make a contribution to the betterment of humankind. So keep your eyes and ears open at all times, Prometheus; the next adventure awaits!

1804 – 1875 Prometheus, June 5 – June 18
1875 – 1946 Prometheus, June 6 – June 19
1946 – 2017 Prometheus, June 7 – June 20
2017 – 2088 Prometheus, June 8 – June 21
2088 – 2159 Prometheus, June 9 – June 22
2159 – 2230 Prometheus, June 10 – June 23

Typhon
June 21 – July 4
6.40 degrees Gemini to 20.00 Gemini

Animal – Dog

Planet - Rahu

For you, Typhon, there is an innate appreciation for the great cycle of destruction and creation. You know deep inside that for the new to emerge, the old must transform or even be destroyed. However, destruction naturally comes first for you, Typhon, because this is how you see things. The old or outmoded must be cleared away so that new structures can arise. As you know from personal experience, things of great worth often grow out of misfortune.

In mythology, Typhon was the god of storms and monsters; and a fearsome creature he was. Part giant, part viper, and part dragon, he seemed to be the original definition of a multiple personality disorder. Those born under this star can also appear to have a couple of personalities and often know first-hand the variety of storms that life can bring. It's not that others don't experience setbacks and disappointments, but the Typhons just seem to have a knack for a unique take on those things. Sometimes they can be the quintessential "lemonade out of lemons" members of the zodiac. At other times, though, they can be anything but.

At their best, a Typhon can regard life's ups and downs with a bemused and knowing look, and a wry or self-deprecating sense of humor is one of the common strengths of the Typhon personality. It's a very necessary part of you, offspring of the storm god, as it not only helps you through the bad times, but also communicates to others the important lessons of those times. Your highly honed communication skills make the difficult palatable, allowing others to laugh at life's challenges though a sense of shared experience.

This is a very fortunate attribute to have, child of Typhon, because you also possess a cold, stubborn streak; and you can be difficult to be around whenever that part of you comes to the fore. But no one can ultimately hold that against you, because at your core, you can be just the kindest person one could ever meet – a tough cookie with a heart of gold.

It goes without saying that you're a fairly complex character, Typhon. You have a real appreciation of the need for change, especially in the form of destruction. Yet you also value the blossoming of new forms; and creation, especially with words, is how many people know you. It's usually only when someone gets particularly close, though, that the complexity of your character can be seen clearly.

Typhon is certainly no stranger to challenge and adversity. Often, a Typhon will have a history of addiction of one sort or another. The pain of understanding the loss involved in destruction, while attempting to extract the creative impulse inherent within it, often exacts a harsh personal toll. Those born of Typhon often fall victim to depression and substance abuse as a common way to deal with this toll.

Along with the appreciation for the depth of destruction necessary for new growth comes a real connection to the personal unconscious. This capacity is not often within the ordinary awareness of Typhons, though, until they do some introspection. For example, harsh, impulsive words spoken in a moment of passion will not be consciously recalled and, in fact, will usually be denied. It isn't that you are trying to cover up, Typhon. You are saying what you believe to be accurate when you deny the hurtful exchange. What happened was actually a blast straight from your unconscious. Those cold jabs, so often stated without awareness, are like bolts of lightning during a very Typhon-like thunder storm. The blast disappears just as quickly, however, leaving a bit of destruction in its wake.

You see, child of Typhon, you can be kind or cruel, optimistic or pessimistic, destructive or creative, victim or victimizer . . . it all depends on your mood and the circumstances. Astrologically, Typhon is completely contained within the sun sign of Gemini, and like anyone born within the bounds of Gemini, you are two modes in one being.

As a result, you may notice people being off balance around you, not knowing which part of you will show up today. You will have to forgive them, though, because often you don't even know what to expect yourself. But you aren't doomed. Typhons that invest their energy in self-discovery and introspection are rewarded with a great deal of control over their destruction/creation personality. When that occurs, tremendous personal growth and wonderful outpourings of creativity result. These results can most easily be seen in the realm of speech. The self-aware Typhon is an effective communicator, shining a light into life's dark corners, and making us all laugh at those things that the old Scottish prayer calls "ghoulies and ghosties, and long-leggedy beasties, and things that go bump in the night."

Being in a relationship with a Typhon individual is no walk in the park. The flashes of their caustic tongue, as well as their tendency toward depression and addiction, make relationships a challenge. Something else that may be difficult for those in relationship with a Typhon is the need that any Typhon has for privacy. That will have to be made clear in the relationship, however. Without alone time, Typhon can become overwhelmed and seek to escape, which may be sought through addiction or depression. This is a strategy that can only be destructive for Typhons and any relationships they are in. Your significant other may not really understand, since they see you in your likeable, happy-go-lucky guise too. Nevertheless, you must insist on your time alone, child of the storm god. Ultimately, your relationship will be the better for it.

Professionally, Typhons often feel the most satisfied in occupations where they can express themselves verbally and persuade others. Teaching, writing, public relations, even stand-up comedy are good examples. On the dark side, however, these same skills can make Typhon a con artist, a drug dealer (. . . or a politician). Seriously, however, it is essential for Typhons to express themselves. Their Gemini-given quickness of mind and mouth must be honored.

To remain healthy, Typhon, you must resist being taken over by your darker tendencies. Over-indulgence in substances, from alcohol and tobacco to sugar and fat, will severely unbalance you, and initiate a destructive cycle from which recovery is difficult. Remember that you must balance the pull toward destruction with that toward creation. Your ability to communicate is among the best in the zodiac, and that can be used for your benefit or detriment. Therefore, paying attention to your self-talk is paramount. Keep careful track of the messages you are sending to yourself. It will give you a good idea about which direction you are headed. Also, be sure to allow time for yourself. It is almost a sacred obligation for you. When you are feeling overwhelmed or stressed, alone time is a must. This is how you rejuvenate. You draw energy from solitude. Don't ever short-change yourself in this regard.

In the pursuit of well-being, strive for balance above all. Both destruction and creation are necessary for evolution. You know that innately, Typhon's child. So watch your tendency to drift toward too much darkness. You may love to wear black, as many born of Typhon do, but that doesn't mean that it needs to be your predominant mood.

The symbol for Typhon is a combination of the diamond and the tear drop. It is an excellent metaphor for the best use of this star's power – to extract the most valuable from the most painful. Meditation on this symbol will be a great source of inspiration for you, Typhon. The animal for this star is the dog, an animal known for its faithfulness in good times and bad. This energy can serve you well through all of life's chapters.

A mixture of light and dark makes those of this star a fascinating part of humanity. Bringing creation out of destruction is one neat trick, but you are capable of it, Typhon; and no one gets greater satisfaction from accomplishing this than you. So bring forth the new and fresh from the old and stale. Plumb the depths to reach the heights. This is your mission, Typhon. Humanity cannot evolve without your contribution.

1804 – 1875 Typhon, June 19 – July 2
1875 – 1946 Typhon, June 20 – July 3
1946 – 2017 Typhon, June 21 – July 4
2017 – 2088 Typhon, June 22 – July 5
2088 – 2159 Typhon, June 23 – July 6
2159 – 2230 Typhon, June 24 – July 7

Artemis
July 5 – July 18
20.00 degrees Gemini to 3.20 Cancer

Animal – Cat

Planet - Jupiter

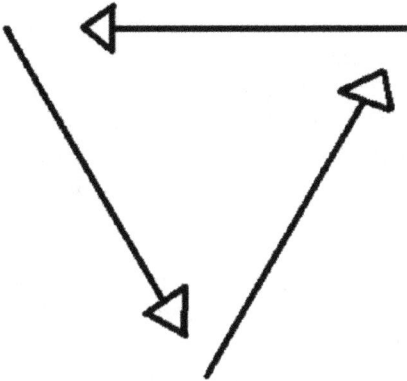

We are all one. That spiritual pronouncement may come as a surprise to some, and provoke doubt in many. But not you, Artemis. That sense of oneness comes to you as naturally as breathing in and out; and in your own way, you would like to convince the world of what you see as a self-evident fact. Perhaps no one has described your sense of the union of everything better than Alan Watts, when he said, "You and I are all at once continuous with the physical universe as a wave is continuous with the ocean." Why can't everyone see this as clearly as you?

The thing is, you have a distinct advantage here. In mythology, Artemis had a tripartite nature – land, sky, and the underworld. On land she was Artemis (Diana to the Romans), the goddess of hunting, animals, and childbirth. She was also known as a great protector of young women. In the sky, she was identified with the moon where she was known by several names, including Selene and Pasiphae (the Romans called her Luna). In the underworld, Artemis became Persephone, bride of Hades (Proserpine was her Roman name). How does this help you in your understanding of the oneness of all? Well, Artemis, you seem to be everywhere, and you are one and the same in all places. This gives you a feeling for every level of existence. With your naturally compassionate nature, identification with others is a snap.

Artemis is a very fortunate star under which to be born. Those born here are blessed with a great level of energy and vitality. You light up a room when you enter. What's more, there is a marked tendency for a quick recovery from anything that saps you. There's a mythological connection here too: Artemis as the huntress carried a quiver of magical arrows that returned to her after their quest was complete. This symbolizes the rapid return of energy so typical of the children of this star.

But there's also a practical side to you, Artemis. You can do quite well in business when you set your mind to it. You have a fine, intuitive (a gift from Luna) business sense that translates into physical action (which you get from Diana) while brooking no resistance (compliments of Proserpine). Also, since the goddess of this star is a protector of women, your desire to work with women tends to be strong. There is often a definite desire to lift women up, and the pursuit of women's rights is frequently a central mission for those born of Artemis.

The children of the Huntress are certainly ambitious. But you believe strongly, Artemis, that dishonesty and subterfuge are not ways to realize your goals. You are honest and forthright to the core, and you are well loved and respected because of it. Others know that you can be depended upon to keep your word and follow through on your promises, which is another trait that can contribute to your success in business.

Now, there will definitely be times when things don't work out for you as planned, Artemis. After all, nobody makes it through life without a few scars. Not to worry, though. Even when it looks like you have lost everything, your amazing inner reserves surface to help you rise again. There's no keeping a good Artemis down!

In the zodiac, this star spans the latter part of Gemini and the earliest degrees of Cancer; and children of Artemis tend to exhibit qualities of both of these sun signs. The residents of Artemis are quick of mind, have a strong intellect, and are gifted communicators, thanks to Gemini. At the same time, they value home and family, are compassionate, and feel strongly for humanity, due to Cancer. You have a nice blend of rationality (the Mercury of Gemini) and intuition (the Moon of Cancer). This blend allows you to find inspiration and make it understandable. This is a knack that brings so many born under Artemis to the written word. Many an Artemis feels a strong urge to put their ideas down on paper, and they often find a publisher eager for their work.

As one born of Artemis, you have high ideals and live by them scrupulously. Having such fervent beliefs, there are times when you feel a strong need to convince others of your point of view. At times like these, an Artemis can become rather insistent, even somewhat pushy. It is important not to be too intense in your efforts, however. Remember, not everyone has your broad vision, nor is everyone capable of understanding it. Allow your example to show the path to realization, Artemis. Fortunately, you won't find this task all that difficult. The star itself enjoys a strong influence from its own ruling planet Jupiter, the planet of good fortune and expansion. People are naturally attracted to you, and are interested in what you have to say. Use this gift with discretion and a kind heart.

Those in a relationship with a child of the Huntress are certainly fortunate as well. Artemis, you are devoted to family and to those close to you. As a result, most born of this star marry, finding a measure of fulfillment in devoting themselves to their spouses and children. You will support and defend them tirelessly, nourishing them when needed and shouldering the burdens when required. Your energy and vitality are infectious, and all who have your love benefit from it.

In line with what has been stated above, consider vocations such as teaching, writing, the entertainment fields, humanitarianism, or even politics. These professions are in line with your natural tendency to show the world your vision. More interested in spiritual things, Artemis, you know that you are not overly attached to the material. Your pursuit of a given career is more for the satisfaction that it brings you. Also, if you can serve women with what you do, so much the better. Artemis is very much in synch with the feminine principle.

However, remember that Artemis is also at home in the business world, particularly when that business enriches the live of others. Artemis knows that when others are lifted up, so are they. One area that can be very rewarding in this regard is the area of wellness. For example, an Artemis can often become intimately involved with a yoga studio, teaching or even owning. This is an excellent fit, naturally meshing with the three-fold aspect of this star's goddess. Yoga seeks union with the Divine (the heavens, Pasiphae) while doing grounding and transformative postures (the underworld, Persephone) which are composed of physically fluid movement (the earth, graceful Artemis). Additionally, the wellness field encourages a belief in the oneness of all, a principle near and dear to the children of this star.

It naturally follows that to keep in the best of health, then, Artemis must pay attention to being well at an all-encompassing, holistic level. The Mercury influence from Gemini can impart sensitivity to the nervous system, a condition that requires calming via a meditation practice. This can be a sitting practice or one that uses graceful motion, such as yoga or tai chi. Artemis must also be sure that the interchange between the inner and outer worlds is flowing and unencumbered. Therefore, breath practices would also be of benefit. Of course, filling the body with unwholesome food can undo the best-planned regimen for spiritual growth. Artemis would be wise to stay close to the land with food choices. The goddess of the hunt and the wilderness does best with an unadulterated, natural diet.

The animal associated with Artemis is the cat, an animal at ease both in nature and in domestication. The cat has long been associated with feminine power, the moon, and the underworld (for example, as a witch's familiar). A graceful hunter, the cat is an ideal animal to symbolize the many facets of this star. As for the symbol of this star, the triangular shape suggests the purpose of arrows, both at rest and in their magical, circular journey from release to return.

Remember, Artemis, the arrow is loosed, straight and true, for a specific purpose. Your clarity, akin to a hunter tracking its quarry, helps guide it on its way. This is how you persuade others regarding your grand, spiritual vision. Use your intuition with single-minded determination. Your words are powerful, your example even more so.

In all your dealings, your natural optimism will be tempered with a realistic appraisal of any potential problems. When your three-part nature is working in harmony, Artemis, you are unbeatable. You become the living embodiment of the oneness of all things.

1804 – 1875 Artemis, July 3 – July 16
1875 – 1946 Artemis, July 4 – July 17
1946 – 2017 Artemis, July 5 – July 18
2017 – 2088 Artemis, July 6 – July 19
2088 – 2159 Artemis, July 7 – July 20
2159 – 2230 Artemis, July 8 – July 21

Zeus

July 19 – August 1

3.20 degrees Cancer to 16.40

Animal – Ram

Planet - Saturn

There aren't many more fortunate than you, child of Zeus. After all, who do you have in your corner but the king of the gods? How can you possibly lose with such a heavy hitter as your ruling deity? You have no trouble spreading your good fortune around, either. It's a driving force for you to assist and uplift all those around you. It's your calling and you embrace it readily.

All this is due to your namesake god. Zeus, called Jupiter by the Romans, was the mythological chief god of the Greeks, and ruler of Mt. Olympus. He was given charge of many areas, including the laws of nature. As such, the weather was one of his realms. With his lightning bolt he nourished the Earth with rain and kept order among those unruly Olympians. He had a lust for life and spent a fair amount of his time procreating. Always willing to share, that Zeus!

Such is the legacy of those born under this star. They feel a strong need to nourish and to share. You are naturally attracted to all things larger than life, Zeus, and your presence is always noticed. You are a person of extremes, and your life circumstances often show it. Looking at the planetary influences of this star makes it all pretty clear.

Lying wholly within the astrological sun sign of Cancer, which is ruled by the Moon, there is a strong lunar influence to this star. From the Moon, the children of Zeus inherit strong emotions, both tender and explosive. The star of Zeus itself is ruled by Saturn, and Zeus corresponds, remember, to the Roman god Jupiter. These are the planets of contraction (Saturn) and expansion (Jupiter). The result is a tendency to exhibit extremes. Zeus, you are often fortunate materially and spiritually. However, there is always the possibility of a setback, a fall from grace. At your best, you are the envy of the zodiac; at your worst, you can be quite a mess.

This is the challenge for you, Zeus. You know that you possess one of the highest natures of all the stars. To be born under Zeus is indeed a boon. Yet, you can be blunted in your endeavors when pride or arrogance blinds you. A humble appreciation for your gifts is the best way to proceed. Deep within you is the knowledge that even when things are at their darkest, you can turn them around. Yeah, you're that good.

You have the ability to achieve tremendous success, perhaps more than any other star in the zodiac. You understand that you can wield tremendous power. Despite this, you have a weakness. You have real trouble with criticism. Zeus, you can become defensively enraged by someone daring to question your course; and even though the lightning bolt of your emotions can come out, you may be left with self-doubt. You have to allow others their opinions, Zeus. Take the information in, and move in the direction you deem best. It tends to work out for you when you do this.

Children of Zeus are very much in touch with emotion and its display. Yes, you can get pretty upset when confronted, Zeus, but you're also kind of a softy. Recall that you are the heart of Cancer the crab, a creature that is hard on the outside but on the inside, not so much. As a result, you can be rather sentimental. That's not a bad thing; this quality helps you in your innate tendency to help and support others. Don't let your sensitivity scare you, even though your natural tendency is to hold some of your emotion inside. Without that sensitivity, you would be much less effective executing your central drive. After all, the truly great always have a blend of leadership and compassion in them. For you, this is a given. Enjoy your softer side as well as your leadership.

The emotional side of you can often bring out a strong, creative streak, Zeus. Indulge it, and let those juices flow. By putting your mind to something, and applying your inborn vibrancy, you often bring about something truly remarkable. Explore wherever those currents lead you. Surprising and satisfying things could result.

At your core, you are very spiritual. Some would say "religious," though you may bristle at the word. However, having the energy of the chief of the gods within you, how could you not be spiritual? Let this energy serve you in your connection with others. You naturally inspire respect and others will seek out your counsel. Remember that your spiritual base is a natural source of nourishment for all who come into contact with you, and the nourishing of others, due to your Cancerian nature, is one of your primary missions in this life.

In relationships, children of Zeus can be a challenge. While they are magnanimous and giving, they can also be proud and volatile, especially when challenged. Also, Zeus was known for "getting around," shall we say. This tendency to stray would have to be kept closely in check for a relationship to be long-lasting. Even though you enjoy family ties, you'll have to face it, Zeus. Your personal magnetism will bring temptation to your door. Many long to be in the presence of dynamism such as yours, and your head could be turned by all that attention. A word to the wise – be aware of the risks before you commit to a relationship. If you have any doubt, it's better to wait rather than jump into something that may only be a flash in the pan.

Your ability to connect with and uplift those around you makes you a natural in the business world. Saturn, the ruling planet of this star, is very much tied to career and business. These two influences can bring you a great deal of business acumen. You have a nice variety of vocations that especially suit your talents. Most positions of leadership inspire you. Since your namesake is a law-giver, look at politics or law enforcement as possibilities. Your creative streak could lead to music or the visual arts. Of course, teaching is another natural vocation for you. Sharing, uplifting, influencing, informing – all the qualities that you and good teachers possess. Finally, with your spiritual core and business nature, you might find yourself attracted to the clergy. Not so unusual, once you realize that the clergy are the businessmen and women of religion and spirituality.

Regarding health, those of Zeus must pay particular attention to the stomach and, for daughters of Zeus, the breasts. Careful attention to diet is a must for those born under this star. With a tendency to go to extremes, Zeus needs to bring conscious awareness to dietary choices. Either too much indulgence or too much austerity is a poor choice to maintain your health, Zeus. Be sensible, and use your sensitivity to assist in the most healthful choices. Listen to others and consider their opinions. In other words, try not to get defensive if your choices are questioned by those near and dear. For exercise, it should be remembered that many children of Zeus are active, athletic, and powerfully built, and would profit from vigorous exercise, with proper medical consultation. Vigorous exercise will also help dissipate excess energy. Do what you enjoy, Zeus, because you are most likely to pursue it faithfully and gain maximum benefit from it. And you are sure to tell everyone about how great it is, sharing as usual.

The animal for this star is the ram. Now, when you are focused on something, Zeus, you could be described as hard-headed, letting nothing stand in your path. Anything that tries is likely to be bowled over if they dare butt heads with you. The strong leadership qualities of the ram also show up frequently in those born under Zeus. The symbol for this star shows a circle (sometimes interpreted as the Moon of Cancer), signifying a lotus blossom. The generous nature of Zeus is reflected here by the rays expanding out from the lotus, the resting place of the gods.

Zeus, you were born to share. Yours is a generous and kind sign, blessed with leadership qualities and a helpful disposition. Consider yourself blessed to be born here, but this propitious birth position requires that you do indeed lift others up, magnanimously sharing your gifts, talents, and abilities for the benefit of all. Inspiration can come to you like a bolt from the blue, not unlike a favorite technique of your namesake. Use this inspiration for the greatest benefit for the greatest number, and your blessings will increase. You will be true to your essential nature, and the world will be better for it.

1804 – 1875 Zeus, July 17 – July 30
1875 – 1946 Zeus, July 18 – July 31
1946 – 2017 Zeus, July 19 – Aug 1
2017 – 2088 Zeus, July 20 – Aug 2
2088 – 2159 Zeus, July 21 – Aug 3
2159 – 2230 Zeus, July 22 – Aug 4

Hydra
August 2 – August 15
16.40 degrees Cancer to 30.00

Animal – Cat

Planet - Mercury

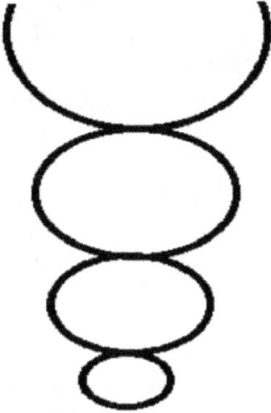

You know what they say about still water – it runs deep. But still water's got nothing on you, Hydra. You are a regular depth merchant. For instance, while we all have our little secrets, you have an entire part of your life that you like to keep close to your vest. And you let nobody, but nobody, inside that place. It's just a part of the complexity that is you.

In mythology, Hydra was the many-headed water serpent that Herakles (a.k.a. Hercules) had to kill as part of his twelve labors. Hydra was a tough one, though, in that every time one of its heads was cut off, it would simply grow back – as two. Herakles saw the futility his approach to this task. He enlisted help in cauterizing the areas of decapitation so that re-growth was impossible, thus defeating the monster.

This many-headed creature shows up in you as a many-faceted nature. You can be very hard to figure out, and many tire themselves out trying. Feeling misunderstood is an occupational hazard of being a Hydra, and any disappointments encountered in your life can become the basis for long-held resentment, even vengeance. As for you, you only want to go about your business unencumbered. Is that too much to ask?

This star is entirely contained within the astrological sun sign of Cancer the crab, which is ruled by the Moon. The planet that rules Hydra itself is Mercury, the planet of quick intelligence, winning speech, and planning. The crab is a creature that loves to hide under rocks, moving stealthily from place to place. It is protected by its hard shell and can give a very painful pinch with its claws when defending itself. Those born of Hydra are very much like this. They can be very secretive and protective, defending parts of themselves with great vigor. They are quick-witted, facile of speech, and intelligent; qualities that help them keep parts of their lives very much their own. However, these same qualities can also make for an adept, destroyer through words, so be careful there, child of the snake.

Hydra, you are "the dark side of the Moon," unknown yet alluring. Many people find you fascinating, and are attracted to what they sense as a mysterious something. And you keep them guessing, Hydra, which leads to either greater attraction or outright rejection on the other's part. But it's all the same to you, Hydra, since you can hide things so well. That is, as long as you aren't hurt by the rejection if it comes. Hydra's children have long memories when it comes to slights either real or imagined, and they can be formidable enemies when aroused. Many have withered under a Hydra's steely-eyed, snake-like stare.

The natural instincts that you have, Hydra, serve you well in the business world. Able to see a problem from many perspectives and intensely competitive, the multi-headed Hydra can be quick to understand even the thorniest of issues. A definite advantage in the work-world, wouldn't you say? Couple that with your innate passion for things you consider important or attractive, and you have a dedicated, some might say relentless, pursuer of any goal. On the other hand, paying attention to too many heads at once can lead to confusion, indecision, worry, fear, and, ultimately, self-doubt. These tendencies reflect the dark side of your Mercury rulership, so keep an eye out for them.

Under it all, though, there is a deeper power that drives you, Hydra. It is the serpent power of kundalini energy. What is that, you ask? Kundalini is a power that allows people to be fully in accord with their higher selves and achieve oneness with Divine Purpose. When properly awakened, and properly respected, kundalini energy can bring about a full functioning of one's considerable gifts. Hydra, you are one of the signs that can contact and use the kundalini energy most readily. But there's a catch. Misused or mishandled, kundalini can be a very destructive force, wreaking havoc not only on you but on those around you. Proper management of this force is essential to your well-being.

You see, here's the thing, Hydra. You know about loss and disappointment. After all, the children of the snake usually have more than their fair share of them, sometimes very early in life. Such occurrences can unwittingly begin unleashing the serpent power of kundalini. Unfortunately, this often happens when one is unprepared for it. The impact of this can make for a fairly dark individual, unless steps are taken to rein in this incredible force. But how to do that?

For one thing, it is important for anyone born of Hydra to have a meditation practice that focuses on the orderly movement of inner forces. Meditations that involve movement, like yoga or qigong, especially those postures which imitate a snake or work with the grounding and rising of spiritual energies, can be quite helpful. Finally, a qualified spiritual teacher can be an immense aid. Strategies like these can keep that unruly kundalini under control if it has awakened, or allow it to awaken gradually if it has not yet done so.

Now, a relationship with a Hydra is a tricky proposition. With your Cancer sun sign, Hydra, there is a part of you that desires the comforts of home and a stable relationship; and you can be considered quite a catch, as many Hydras are confident, alluring, and sexually enticing. However, the dark, secretive side of you will make for potential trouble in any relationship. Sometimes, the secret side of Hydra includes an addiction of some sort, for example, substances, sex, or gambling. Needless to say, this does not make for a happy relationship; and your tendency to strike out at those who would intrude on your privacy only adds to the problem. Any romantic partner you have must be tolerant of your need to have some part of you that is completely and secretly yours. Needless to say, that secret part can't be inherently at odds with maintaining a good relationship. All in all, it may be a tough order to fill.

Vocationally, Hydra has a wide field of potentially satisfying careers. With your acute business sense and incisive mind, you could find satisfaction in a number of professions, from politics and the law to teacher and inventor. Also, don't forget the mystical professions, such as astrology. Your contact with kundalini lends a decidedly mystical flair to your personality, and you can find deep fulfillment in those vocations, if you are interested. However, what must be kept in check, Hydra, is the temptation to want to swallow things whole, just like a snake. Taking in too much oftentimes ignites greed or a grasping neediness, faults that Hydra can fall victim to very easily.

For living healthily, Hydras must mind their diet and choices of food. Snakes take in quite a bit when they feed, and then remain relatively inert while digestion takes place. Indiscretion in food choice can lead to a good bit of digestive trouble for you, Hydra. Please keep your eyes smaller than your stomach. Also, your Mercury ruler can bring about a sensitive nervous system, so be sure to take time to be kind to yourself. Meditation and movement practices, such as those mentioned above, will calm the nervous system and help rein in that infamous temper of yours; not to mention maintaining limberness in your joints, thereby keeping arthritis and the creakiness of aging at bay. Additionally, there's nothing wrong with your holding onto a bit of yourself for yourself. Mastering that need, while making sure that it is destructive to no one, can bring you an inner sense of peace. It can be a secure and nurturing practice to cultivate.

The animal assigned to this star is the cat. Think of a tomcat, strutting his stuff in the darkness. A formidable foe, a canny hunter, popular with the ladies – all of these things invoke Hydra. But use the power inherent in this animal without falling victim to hubris or uncontrolled emotion. Properly appreciated, the cat a powerful metaphor for you, child of Hydra. The symbol for this star suggests two entwining snakes, like the DNA helix, the scepter of Mercury, or the circulating chakra currents activated by kundalini. This symbol can remind you, Hydra, of your power to activate mystical energies and to use them for evolutionary change or original ideas.

Hydra, you have chosen a challenging life. You can light up the universe or crash in flames. It all comes down to how you choose to handle the force with which you have an intimate, innate connection. Use your strong, incisive reasoning powers and talent for convincing speech wisely. Understand that you are influential and can be held in high esteem. But keep some secrets, Hydra. It is what gives you your appeal, and what brings you security and peace. Reach for the stars, Hydra. If anyone can hold them fast, it is you.

1804 – 1875 Hydra, July 31 – Aug 13
1875 – 1946 Hydra, Aug 1 – Aug 14
1946 – 2017 Hydra, Aug 2 – Aug 15
2017 – 2088 Hydra, Aug 3 – Aug 16
2088 – 2159 Hydra, Aug 4 – Aug 17
2159 – 2230 Hydra, Aug 5 – Aug 18

Persephone
August 16 – August 29
00.0 degrees Leo to 13.20

Animal – Rat

Planet - Ketu

Shakespeare could have been thinking about you, Persephone, when he wrote, "Some are born great, some achieve greatness, and some have greatness thrust upon them." Frankly, you can manifest in any of these ways. Greatness, in some form or another, is often the hallmark of those born under this star.

In Greek mythology Persephone is probably best known as queen of the underworld. Bride of Hades, she spent part of the year with him, but she also spent time "above ground" as Core, goddess of spring. She ruled, therefore, over the grandeur of nature, and over the realm of the dead. Either way, she was a ruler.

This is often the fate of those born of Persephone. Greatness and leadership attract them, and they feel quite at home being in charge and organizing things. However, there is an interesting split within this sign. Some children of Persephone are more like the spring goddess, likable and light, wanting to uplift. Others are more like the queen of the underworld, eccentric and serious, often pursuing power and control. In both cases, there is competence and confidence in their ability to lead, and frequently, many people are more than willing to follow them.

Persephone, you are the stuff of kings, queens, and presidents. Though you may never aspire to public office, you instinctively know that you were born to take charge. There is usually a tangible, noble quality to Persephone's children. They have a fortunate, gifted air about them; they are often rather charismatic as well.

Of course, there is a dark side to all of this. As is said, "Pride goeth before the fall." Therein lies your shortcoming, Persephone. If you get too impressed with yourself, allowing pride or arrogance to take control, you will surely fall from grace, and fall hard. This may not prevent you from rising again, but the journey back is usually tough, and dining on crow is a common occurrence during that return to glory.

The star of Persephone lies entirely within the astrological sun sign of Leo, which is ruled by the powerful Sun; and those born of this sign leave no doubt about that. They carry themselves in a regal manner, and expect to be treated as a cut above the ordinary. This influences the way you interact with others. At your best, Persephone, you are magnanimous, kind, giving, and the epitome of a great leader. At your worst, you can resemble a petty tyrant.

However, one thing that you often have going for you, Persephone, is your respect for what came before. Many of Persephone's children are very aware of the contributions of their ancestors, and they respect tradition, perhaps even to the extent of being regarded as overly conservative. Don't let that bother you. You know instinctively that tradition has a purpose, and there's nothing wrong with honoring that. In fact, your confident self might just start of few of your own. And who better, you might ask yourself rhetorically?

Persephone is often quite comfortable in the world of business. Her children are often go-getters, those who are looking to lead and to organize effort. You are not one to shrink from that kind of responsibility, Persephone. It comes pretty easily to you, taking charge and delegating when necessary. Like any good leader, you are an able recognizer of talent and know how to put it all to good use. One obstacle you may have to overcome, though, is that you may not look the part. Persephone's children are not necessarily flashy of manner (there's that love of tradition again), and therefore can be underestimated by others. Now, any Persephone knows that this underestimation can be used to great advantage. Many battlefields, both actual and figurative, are littered with the remains of those who dared to underestimate you. While not really savage, you are nevertheless cunning and resourceful. This is how you come out on top.

Few things are more exciting to a child of Persephone than a business challenge. Knowing and respecting the past, you can understand how to transform old patterns into more effective forms. You want to explore, and you tend to be fearless. You can't control what you fear, so an avoidant course of action simply won't do. Stretching your edges suits you just fine, Persephone. How else are you going to grow, and possibly extend the realm of your control?

Vocationally, Persephones can find satisfaction in any profession where they are able to lead, organize, or direct. Politics is an obvious choice, but areas such as the law will also work well. Your interest in tradition and the past could lead you into fields like history or archeology. The arts may also beckon, and a Persephone would find themselves quite happy in the visual arts or music (obviously aiming toward being first chair, or even the conductor of an orchestra). In any endeavor, Persephone, you would probably be more satisfied in a position where you call the shots, as anything from project leader to being self-employed in some capacity. However, pride or arrogance could also be your undoing here. Expecting to be recognized as innately superior, so that everything will be handed to you, is a recipe for disappointment. Laziness doesn't look good on you.

Interestingly enough, Persephone also has a mystical side. It's as if you recognize the power of the unseen. This attraction no doubt comes from Persephone's rulership of the underworld. However, another influence here is the fact that the planet that rules the star of Persephone is the mystical South Node of the Moon. This is also known as Cauda Draconis (the Dragon's Tail), or by its Hindu name of Ketu. While not an actual, physical planet, the South Node nevertheless has a significant impact on those born under its influence. As a result of these powerful associations, children of Persephone commonly have an interest in matters like ghosts and hauntings. Feel free to indulge this side of yourself, Persephone. It satisfies a deep connection within you, though possibly more strongly if you are the "underworld" kind of Persephone as opposed to the "spring" version of the sign.

The world of relationships can be a challenge for you, Persephone, as it can easily become a struggle for power. Granted, with your love of a challenge, you might not want to partner with someone who will cede the power aspect of a relationship to you too easily. However, constantly struggling over who's in charge is tiresome, and it certainly isn't conducive to pleasant interactions. Just like in business, then, some negotiation will be necessary for success on the relationship front. If you can find a partner who is willing to work with you for the common benefit of all, you have found a winner.

In the realm of health, it is important for Persephone's children to work to calm their natural intensity so that they can use it constructively, rather than have it control them. With this in mind, calming practices like meditation will be useful. Also, due to the association of this sign with nature, time spent there occupied with peaceful pursuits, will bear great dividends. Stress is often a problem, and Persephone would be wise to develop a number of strategies for dealing with it. Diet should be relatively simple, heart healthy (remember Leo rules the heart), and natural. Be alert for signs of high stress, like hypertension or gastric distress, and act to curb them. The worst thing you could do for your health, Persephone, is to let your natural pride get in the way. If you need assistance or guidance in the area of health, get it. Don't let prideful denial lead you into a problem.

Not surprisingly, the symbol for this star is a crown! Was there any doubt? The crown matches your bearing and your natural leadership abilities. However, this crown is not ornate. As such, it can serve as a reminder that the best leader is one who is compassionate and approachable, not tyrannical. The animal associated with this star is the rat. Doesn't seem very regal, does it? Well, the point of the rat's association lies in its cleverness and resourcefulness, as well as its perseverance at gnawing through any obstacle in its path. These qualities are ones that you possess and can easily access, Persephone. Remember, the rat is a survivor, unafraid and cunning. Emulating the rat in this regard is your innate tendency. Honor it and use it for your benefit.

Persephone, never forget that the world needs your talents and gifts. Providing direction for maximal effectiveness; leading in uncertain times; preserving links to the past and respected traditions – these are all gifts that you bring to humanity. You are the joyous outburst of the energy of the goddess of spring and the deep, sure leadership of the queen of the underworld. Where would the world be without you?

1804 – 1875 Persephone, Aug 14 – Aug 27
1875 – 1946 Persephone, Aug 15 – Aug 28
1946 – 2017 Persephone, Aug 16 – Aug 29
2017 – 2088 Persephone, Aug 17 – Aug 30
2088 – 2159 Persephone, Aug 18 – Sept 1
2159 – 2230 Persephone, Aug 19 – Sept 2

Bacchus

August 30 – September 12
13.20 degrees Leo to 26.40

Animal – Mink

Planet - Venus

Bacchus, at first glance some might think that your sign is a bit trivial – god of wine, and all that. But nothing could be further from the truth. You already know it, but if others expect you to be a superficial party animal, they've got another thing coming.

In mythology, Bacchus (Dionysius in Greek) was indeed the god of wine and good times. But Bacchus traditionally held a much deeper understanding of the sense of intoxication as well; in essence, intoxication with the Divine. Children of Bacchus tend to be very much in touch with the ecstasy that a true communion with higher energies can give. They naturally flow with that energy, and as it flows through them, they become examples of this sublime bliss for the rest of humanity.

The typical Bacchus sounds like someone everyone could use in their lives. They are a kind and loyal group, and lift others up with their natural sense of joy and their positive outlook. They tend to be quite kind. They are affectionate to those close to them, and they are steadfast defenders of them, too. In other words, Bacchus, you are definitely the go-to person for loyalty and generosity.

The star of Bacchus lies entirely within the sun sign of Leo. In fact, Bacchus can be seen as the heart of the lion, and this fact imparts a unique quality to those born here. The heart-centered children of Bacchus have a strong attachment to their emotions. Thus, they may not strike everyone as "a typical Leo." It's true, Bacchus. You certainly are softer in your approach to life and relationships than many born under the sign of the lion. Perhaps it is because Bacchus itself is ruled by Venus, the planet of emotion, sensitivity, love, and beauty.

Venus certainly leaves her mark on the children of Bacchus, as they tend to be attractive, sensual, influential, and beguiling. Bacchus, you love to love and you love to be in appealing surroundings. You also have a natural artistic and creative flair that you bring to all your endeavors. It's in your nature to know when something is not quite right, and you are driven to fix it.

However, here's where you can run into trouble, child of the lion. Sometimes you can become controlling, since you see what needs to be done and you will want to move the process along. After all, you are orderly in your own life and you take pains to present yourself attractively, don't you? You keep yourself and your spaces clean and tidy, very much a tribute to your Venusian ruler. So, naturally you have a desire to do the same for others. Taken to extremes, though, your inner "control freak" can come out, and cause conflict with others. Best to let things take their own course sometimes, Bacchus. You know how it is – there are times when people just have to learn at their own rate, gradually discovering what you have known all along. Gentle prompting is in order, not issuing edicts that must be followed. There are times when the most judicious course of action is to keep the taskmaster in you under control. Discernment is the key, Bacchus.

Bacchus is a lion, that's for sure; in particular, a female lion. Why the lioness? It's because of your ability to do it all, Bacchus, and to carry it off with a seeming sense of ease. In the lion's pride, it is the female that takes care of the day-to-day tasks. She is a competent, caring parent, a provider of food, and the glue that keeps the group a cohesive whole. The "femaleness" of this is, in part, the influence of Venus. But make no mistake. Bacchus is all lion, and to cross a Bacchus can be a large misstep.

By its very makeup, this star is associated with a strong sense of nurturance, and any Bacchus is a born nurturer. However, never forget that there is the fierceness of the lion underneath. Translation: sometimes you get a hug from Bacchus, sometimes you get swatted up side the head with a strong paw – and all in the name of nurturance. Bacchus, you instinctively know what is needed and you do what is best to help others grow. Meanwhile, your excellent communication skills minimize misunderstanding. Be it carrot or stick, Bacchus, the choice is yours, and your instincts will serve you surely and easily in your decision.

Something to be careful of, Bacchus, is the fact that your deep discernment of what another might need can lead to fault-finding. You have a perfectionistic streak in you, and anything that isn't quite right can really get under your skin. This is as true when it comes to people as it is for your surroundings. People are tricky, though, and may not take kindly to your suggestions and corrections. Here's where you can learn a great lesson, Bacchus. To deal with fault-finding, you will have to resort to another f-word: forgiveness. As was said before, sometimes it's simply best to let things take their own course and allow people to grow, possibly through your example rather than your criticism. It seems paradoxical, but there are times when letting things be, in a spirit of forgiveness, will lead to fuller and more lasting change than using direct interventions.

There is, as always, a dark side to this desire to correct that which is out of alignment. You have a strong pull within you to take on the burdens of others, absorbing their challenging energies in an attempt to bring order. It's all part of the natural interchange you undergo while in contact with others, especially if they are feeling needy. You are such a nurturer, Bacchus, that you constantly seek to assist; and there's a part of you that knows how strong you really are. Nevertheless, taking on too much of the energy of others can wear you down. You have to learn when to refuse the burden and just take care of yourself.

Still in all, Bacchus is about interactions with others, and most of the time there is nothing more special than being in a relationship. Bacchus, you are natural marriage material, and most of those born under this star find fulfillment within marriage and family. Here your deepest tendencies can be given free rein, and you bring success to those who truly wish for it and work for it. Your lioness self will make sure that the home is well kept and orderly, and that no one in it will suffer from a lack of love. You will be tough but fair, and sure that no one slacks in his or her work, physically or spiritually.

Vocationally, Bacchus does best in positions of authority, autonomy, and control (no surprise there). When placed in a one-down position, Bacchus can bristle and those higher up the food chain often feel the discontent that comes with the suppression of a Bacchus's natural drive to lead. Self-employment suits Bacchus well, though any position where project direction is needed provides a nice fit for those of this star. Their strong affiliation with the emotional realm can also give Bacchus satisfaction as an artist or therapist. When the leadership drive is particularly strong, Bacchus may gravitate toward politics or teaching. With that talent for relationships, some of this star can even feel particularly comfortable as a wedding planner or relationship counselor. Many talents, many possibilities for those born of Bacchus.

One would think that all this nurturing and care-taking, which often results in taking on the burdens and problematic energies of others, would take its toll. And it does, Bacchus, it certainly does. You could easily find yourself becoming fatigued or burnt out, and becoming fretful over small or insignificant things. At times like these, your temper can be on edge. Regular rest, even in the form of a daily nap, is important for you. Take a lesson from the lioness, and see how she behaves. She takes care of all her responsibilities, but makes sure to get her rest.

Leo is a fire sign, so Bacchus needs to take care with becoming too fiery, which could lead to problems with the heart or with circulation. Rest and stress management become very important for this reason as well. Strong communicators, it would stand to reason that a good stress management strategy for Bacchus would involve breathing and the voice. Practices in breath control, such as pranayama or deep breathing, can be beneficial. Chanting is also a wonderful aid for Bacchus, using the breath and voice, while calling forth that Divine intoxication which is the special gift of this sign.

The animal associated with Bacchus is the mink. Sensuous, sinewy, and the mark of royalty, this animal embodies many qualities of the children of the lion. The mink also symbolizes the ability to be in the physical and spiritual worlds with joy and a playful attitude. You would be wise to take these lessons to heart (pun intended), Bacchus. The symbol for this sign suggests the hammock, with its calm and gentle rhythms. This symbol also is associated with a peaceful home and pleasant relationships.

Wield your awesome power wisely, Bacchus. Heart of the lion, you are so many things. You are the support for many productive relationships. You are courageous and caring, a source of strength and nurturance. You lift others up and show them the way, while making sure that they know the consequences of their actions. When you roar, some quake, yet many are reassured. Dance with the bliss of divine intoxication, Bacchus. Lead the way.

1804 – 1875 Bacchus, Aug 28 – Sept 10
1875 – 1946 Bacchus, Aug 29 – Sept 11
1946 – 2017 Bacchus, Aug 30 – Sept 12
2017 – 2088 Bacchus, Sept 1 – Sept 13
2088 – 2159 Bacchus, Sept 2 – Sept 14
2159 – 2230 Bacchus, Sept 3 – Sept 15

Hymenaeus
September 13 – September 25
26.40 degrees Leo to 10.00 Virgo

Animal – Bull

Planet - Sun

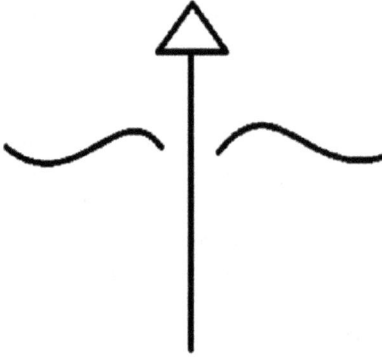

For you, Hymenaeus, it's all about harmony. You love it when things align and relationships are moving swimmingly along. Actually, you are the agent for much of the harmony you see around you. It is central to who you are.

To be completely honest, the use of the word "harmony" is very purposeful. In mythology, Hymenaeus was a young man who was one of the gods of love and song. He was always linked with marriage, and the wedding song of old was named for him. One myth about him involves his daring all for love, saving young maidens who had been kidnapped by robbers. In exchange, he was given the hand of his beloved, which resulted in a long and very happy marriage. Traditionally, invoking Hymenaeus at the beginning of a marriage was a request for bliss throughout a couple's time together.

Like Bacchus before you, Hymenaeus, you naturally gravitate toward committed relationships and married life. A good relationship is at the core of what holds the greatest meaning for you, and like your namesake god, you will dare all to achieve it. This makes you a fine and devoted mate, faithful and true. Those born of this star tend to be cheerful, kind, and friendly. Stable and consistent, they are willing to put others before themselves if need be. Additionally, they are not afraid to stand up for what they see as the right thing to do. Hymenaeus, you can be very courageous indeed, a standout in the name of your beliefs, and a stalwart champion of the oppressed.

This star spans two sun signs, the latter part of Leo and the beginning of Virgo. Therefore, the qualities of Hymenaeus blend aspects of them both. The best emotional aspects of Leo are magnanimity and cheerfulness, and these are right up your alley, Hymenaeus. You naturally tend to look on the bright side, as the sun rules your star as well as the sign of Leo. Affable and cheerful, with an almost child-like expectation of the best in most situations. This is the effect of the double-sun influence of Hymenaeus. Leo is also where you get your ability to take a courageous stance.

The Virgo side of Hymenaeus can keep you from getting too arrogant. Virgo is a sign of service, and you certainly devote yourself to those you love, as well as the downtrodden and needy. Virgo is ruled by thoughtful Mercury, which results in the ability to be considerate and to see the viewpoint of others. This is Hymenaeus at its best, a perfect blend of openness and caring.

Paying special attention to your relationships, Hymenaeus, has another payoff besides enjoyable interactions and physical fulfillment. It is nothing short of your road to spiritual advancement. Those born under this star can progress at all levels, from the physical to the spiritual, by making and keeping a good relationship. The recognition of the Divine in the other is a hallmark of a spiritually evolved relationship. Hymenaeus, this is something that comes to you naturally when you open up to it. The results can be nothing less than fantastic. It would be wise to cultivate this attitude of Divine recognition in your dealings with others.

But there is a dark side as well. Nothing worth achieving is without one, you know. So what is this dark side? Well, Hymenaeus, if you aren't careful, you can become a first-class martyr to love. Daring all is one thing; sacrificing your very self is quite another. This all comes from the negative aspects of the sun signs that Hymenaeus crosses. For example, Leo's cheerfulness can lead to the donning of rose colored glasses. Any idealization of the other can lead to the denial or underplaying of problems in the relationship. As a result, you can be caught in the trap of giving and giving without receiving. This inevitably leads to your becoming exhausted by the relationship, a very unhappy place to be. A negative Virgo influence leads to a stance of denying yourself and becoming a servant – another way of being used in a relationship. This dynamic may also play out, Hymenaeus, as one in which you are tempted to control the other, so that they conform to your specific ideas of what is special or perfect in a relationship. On the other extreme, you may become overly dependent on the other, placing yourself in a very vulnerable position.

The likely outcome of any of these scenarios is that you will become resentful, child of Hymenaeus. Resentful, angry, dissatisfied, even vengeful (a wounded Leo is not a pretty sight). When a bad relationship breaks up, as it almost inevitably will, so will any illusion you have harbored about it. At worst, Hymenaeus, you can be tempted to obsess about the other, to continue to idealize them, or even to stalk them. Things can go to the other extreme, though, and can manifest as intense hatred of the other, or even of yourself for having "failed" at the quest so central to your purpose in life.

As you can see, Hymenaeus, the stakes are high. The rewards of a successful relationship are great, but so are the consequences if taken to the other extreme. In part, this may come from over-emphasizing the necessity of being in a relationship constantly. Almost certainly, there will be times, Hymenaeus, when you will be alone. There may be a real pull to feeling upset and disgruntled when this occurs. But herein lies your challenge. You must learn to embrace aloneness without feeling lonely, Hymenaeus. After all, the most central relationship in life is the one you have with yourself. Get that one into good shape and any others will be that much better.

Vocationally, the natural courage and optimism of this sign can bring about a great deal of satisfaction in a career. Hymenaeus may find itself drawn to a wide variety of fields where contact with people is involved. Social work, the healing arts, philanthropy, music, acting, even public service as a government employee are all good possibilities for the devoted child of Hymenaeus. The key aspect is involvement with people. Your natural talents for relationship, along with your steadfast ways of focusing on a goal, can bring you fulfillment in many areas.

The health of a Hymenaeus may be positively influenced by taking special care of those areas associated with physical contact and relationships, namely the skin, particularly the lips, and the sexual organs. Care not to over-expose oneself to the sun, proper cleanliness, and attention to sexually transmitted disease prevention are all important. The Virgo influence in you can lead to finicky digestion, Hymenaeus, so attention to diet is a must as well. Also, with your spiritual advancement in mind, meditation is key. A meditation practice will help you develop a good relationship with yourself and with your inner strength. This is so very important in the development of strong and healthy relationships with others.

The animal associated with Hymenaeus is the bull, a creature associated with steadfastness, service, and faithfulness, but also with stubbornness and rigidity of belief. With the discernment of Mercury, you can discover when each of these qualities is most appropriate, Hymenaeus. The symbol for this sign is the arrow of the sunrise, all the wiser for having a higher perspective. Perhaps one can imagine the curves below the arrow representing the hair of Virgo, the virgin. In this way, the symbol unites the sun signs where Hymenaeus lies.

You can show the world the beauty that a good and fulfilling relationship is, Hymenaeus. Optimistic and friendly, courageous and devoted, you provide an inspiration for all of humanity. Your purpose is to show humankind how to exist together in harmony, how to love, and how to take care of one another. Hymenaeus, sing your song of love fearlessly, for the world needs to hear it!

1804 – 1875 Hymenaeus, Sept 11 – Sept 23
1875 – 1946 Hymenaeus, Sept 12 – Sept 24
1946 – 2017 Hymenaeus, Sept 13 – Sept 25
2017 – 2088 Hymenaeus, Sept 14 – Sept 26
2088 – 2159 Hymenaeus, Sept 15 – Sept 27
2159 – 2230 Hymenaeus, Sept 16 – Sept 28

Sol
September 26 – October 12
10.00 degrees Virgo to 23.20

Animal – Buffalo

Planet - Moon

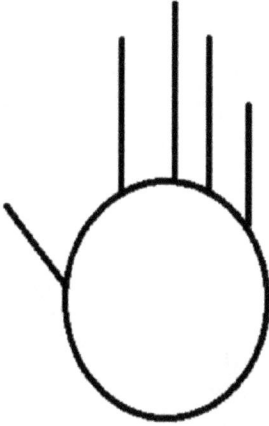

The universe would like to give you a big hand, Sol, because you are always so ready to lend one to others. It's true that if you were born under this star, anything that involves the use of the hand may come very easily for you. Helping, creating, healing – it's all part of this star's legacy.

Named for the Titan god of the Sun, Sol was imagined as the charioteer who would drive his steeds across the sky each day, giving light and life to the Earth. He would rise for his daily round from the river Oceanus, the world ocean that encircled all the lands of the planet. In the evening, he reached the place of the Hesperides, the western nymphs. Here, he would descend, following the currents of Oceanus back to his eastern home.

The grouping of stars associated with Sol form the shape of a hand in the sky. As a result, Sol is associated with the human hand and all of its abilities. Children of Sol are gifted in manual arts, such as various crafts, and in healing methods that use the hand, such as massage.

Additionally, Sol lies entirely within the sun sign of Virgo, the virgin. Virgo is ruled by Mercury, while Sol itself is ruled by the Moon. This combination gives those born here some enviable gifts. Mercury is the planet of communication and mental analysis, while the Moon lends a creative and emotional flavor. Spin these two influences together and you get someone who is often witty, humorous, approachable, and a clever talker. Comfortable with analysis, due to the Mercury connection, Sol's children can be intelligent, deep thinkers. Also, original ideas can often spring forth from their fertile, Moon-tinged imaginations.

Your namesake god was the ultimate follower of routine, Sol. Every day, the same thing. Up at the crack of dawn (come to think of it, he *was* the crack of dawn), drive the chariot across the sky, settle down into the West, and then ride the currents back home. Perhaps that's why you are so comfortable with routines yourself. But, there may be an even more compelling reason. Children of Sol often experience hardship or trauma early in life, anything from poverty to abuse to the death of a parent. Under such circumstances, routine and safety are welcome protection in a seemingly random or out of control world. Cravings for the humdrum would be an understandable outcome of these early experiences.

An inherent sense of helpfulness is also common to those of this star. With the Moon's gift of empathy, and the healing inclinations of Virgo, Sol's children often find themselves in situations where they can, literally or figuratively, lend a helping hand. And they do. In fact, it's not uncommon, Sol, for you to dedicate your life to the service of others. It is easy for you to understand the suffering of other people, no doubt due to the empathy derived from any childhood difficulties you may have endured.

Another result of these frequently difficult early life experiences is a turning toward spirituality, settling on a group of beliefs or values that are held tightly; and those born of this star can certainly hold on tightly, sometimes to the point of being stubborn or immovable. Regardless, Sol, you are one of the more spiritual stars, and this often brings great dividends. Interestingly enough, however, this overt spiritual turning is more common in men born under this star. Women more often try their hand (pun intended) at a variety of things – giving back, helping, and sometimes becoming a jack-of-all-trades. This can often be another mode of spiritual expression, though care needs to be taken that this spreading of energy doesn't lead to a lack of groundedness. Nevertheless, both paths seem to be a way of bringing sense to the unpredictable life that those born of this star may have undergone as youngsters.

Unfortunately, not all of Sol's children take a helpful or spiritual turn. Those who cannot channel the painful emotions of youth in an appropriate manner may turn to unsavory pursuits. Thievery (Sol can be a natural pickpocket) and confidence schemes (a quick wit and fast-talking style) can result when Sol turns to the dark side. Temptations in this direction must obviously be resisted. Keeping your spiritual side healthy and vibrant, Sol, is the way around these potential pitfalls.

Relationships with someone born under Sol would seem to be pretty ideal. Sol is a partner that is quite empathetic and caring. As a result, there is a strong sense of giving and sacrifice for the other in a relationship. As long as this tendency for sacrifice is kept from going overboard, and the other is responsive enough to give as well, balance can be maintained. This contributes to a strong sense of satisfaction and a solid base on which to build a satisfying relationship.

But, of course, there can be problems in relationships, and for you, Sol, these mostly revolve around your Virgo nature. How so? Remember that Virgo is a communicative sign, ruled by chatty Mercury. As a result, there is a great deal of emphasis on verbal communication. It is too easy for you to over-communicate, talking too long and too much, repeating yourself, thereby beating the proverbial dead horse. Coupled with that sense of self-sacrifice (from an overly sensitive Moon), this tendency can lead to someone who needs constant communication and reassurance. Such a smothering approach can snuff out the flames of any relationship, so be very careful here. You must learn the limits of another's tolerance for verbal interaction and respect it. Very few have the need or the desire to "talk it out" as much as you. Sometimes, once said is enough.

Vocationally, the choices are many for someone born under this star. As has been said, Sol, you are handy, in many ways. This could express itself in crafts and craftsmanship, or in the healing professions, especially those that specifically utilize the skill of the hand, such as massage, physical therapy, surgery, or chiropractic. The Moon's rulership brings a compassionate, kind aspect into play, an asset in many of these fields. However, the Moon also has a psychic influence and Sol can find satisfaction in occult areas as an astrologer or a palm reader, fields requiring the analytical strength of Mercury. After all, who better to read the messages of the hand than one of Sol's offspring?

Communicating with others is another strength (remember that Virgo Mercury!). Therefore, careers in sales, writing, public relations, or fields that require careful analysis are all good possibilities. Teaching is another fine choice, combining the Moon's compassion and Mercury's communication. So many choices, Sol. What strikes your fancy?

Regarding health and well-being, those of this star have a few challenges. Virgo is one of the most sensitive signs for health concerns, especially in the digestive tract. Therefore, Sol, be particularly aware of diet and what works or does not work for you digestively. Proper elimination is a must, especially for those with a Virgo sun sign, so be sure that your bowels remain regular. The skin is another very important eliminative organ. Sol, with its hyper-awareness in the very sensitive skin area of the hand, is vulnerable here too. Beware of skin infections and irritations. Take great care to avoid too much sun exposure and allergens.

Mercury, for all its analytical strength, has the drawback of bestowing a sensitive nervous system. As a result, meditation is extremely important to quiet the very active mind of anyone born of this star. Finally, forgiveness is a powerful medicine, and Sol can benefit from this by letting go of incidents that may have been upsetting in childhood. As you forgive, Sol, you reclaim energy that was stuck in the past, freeing up resources for you to use in your spiritual quest.

Sol is symbolized by a human hand, which matches quite nicely with its formation in the heavens. Another traditional symbol is the potter's wheel, which also suggests the craft mastery attainable by members of this sign. The animal associated with Sol is the buffalo, a strong and determined creature. This reminds those of this sign of their strength of resolution, and their ability to persevere through adversity – but also of their tendency toward stubbornness and grudge holding.

Sol, you are insightful, intelligent, and good with your hands. All of these gifts can be used to improve the lot of humanity and allow you to focus on that which is most important, your progress in spiritual development. Whatever your chosen path, you can't go wrong if you keep your eyes set on that ultimate prize. Your naturally compassionate and helpful spirit can guide you and those whose lives you touch along the most important road there is. Most significantly, if you use your considerable skills wisely, the key to your enlightenment will be right in the palm of your hand!

1804 – 1875 Sol, Sept 24 – Oct 10
1875 – 1946 Sol, Sept 25 – Oct 11
1946 – 2017 Sol, Sept 26 – Oct 12
2017 – 2088 Sol, Sept 27 – Oct 13
2088 – 2159 Sol, Sept 28 – Oct 14
2159 – 2230 Sol, Sept 29 – Oct 15

Vulcan

October 13 – October 22
23.20 degrees Virgo to 6.40 Libra

Animal – Tiger

Planet - Mars

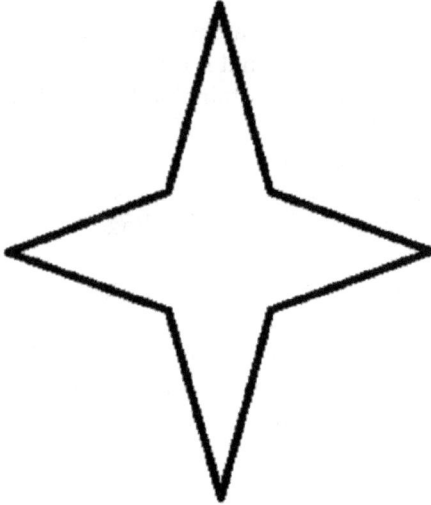

Vulcan, you make an impression wherever you go. Whether it be your soft, alluring eyes, your stylish, well accessorized wardrobe, or your clever, captivating conversation, you are hard to forget. Your gift to the world is your natural sense of design and organization.

In mythology, Vulcan is the god of fire and the forge. He manifested in the natural occurrences of fire and volcanism. Through his strength, landforms changed and metal was molded into shapes both pleasing and deadly. He was the patron of smiths and forgers of metal, even jewelers and sculptors. He had a vengeful streak, however, and never forgot a slight. His judgment was harsh when rendered.

The sign of Vulcan is closely associated with the blue-white star Spica in the constellation Virgo. This star is very bright and displays a variety of colors in its twinkling. This is you, child of Vulcan. You delight in colors and sparkling ornamentation, both on your person and in your surroundings. You can also show yourself personally in a variety of lights. Not surprising, given the three planets at play in your sign.

Vulcan spans two solar signs, the last part of Virgo and the first part of Libra, ruled by Mercury and Venus respectively. The sign of Vulcan itself is ruled by fiery Mars. The combination of energies here is impressive. Mercury gives quick thinking and communication skill, Venus brings an appreciation for beauty and order, while Mars provides the underlying energy and drive. The result is that those born of this star often draw attention to themselves in various ways.

When Mercury holds sway, children of Vulcan can be spell-binding conversationalists, seducing others with the power of their words. If Venus steps to the fore, an artistic streak shows itself, and Vulcans can be accomplished in the arts, in the organization of spaces, or in bringing harmony to disparate forces. Meanwhile, Mars provides the push or passion for these pursuits, Vulcan, making your position irresistible. The fact that those of this star are often blessed with an attractive manner or appearance certainly doesn't hurt either.

But all of this can go to your head, and this is where trouble results. Remember, Vulcan, that your namesake god could be quite judgmental and carry a grudge. Granted, a discriminating eye and exacting taste are important for making design decisions. However, when applied to people, this can come across as a tendency to judge others harshly, even callously. If you feel that others are avoiding you, this is why. The children of Vulcan can be difficult to be around, especially when the judgment goggles come out. You may have some valid points, but understanding the motivations of others will help you keep your judgmental side in check. Also, tact is of the essence when dispensing your (sometimes unwelcome) observations. How many times have you spoken in haste, only to wish that you could take it all back a few hours later? It is essential to realize that cultivating self-awareness and using the gifts of Mercury and Venus to craft appealing statements can go a long way toward avoiding unpleasant and unnecessary interactions.

At worst, the tendencies talked about above can lead to a sort of victim consciousness. Harsh judgment easily gives way to blame of others when situations are not to Vulcan's liking. When others are at fault, disagreements and misunderstandings become fuel for feeling wronged or unappreciated. In times like these, the victim enters. Be careful when that happens. Victimhood is neither attractive nor productive.

Perhaps the greatest work for those born of Vulcan is learning mastery of the ego. The gifts are many for those born under this star. It's so easy for the ego to take control, resulting in an arrogant person, smug and self-satisfied. When that is the case, verbal exchanges can be short, hurtful, and extremely judgmental. A double standard also can develop, leading to a self-indulgent individual. Slights are seen as the jealousy of others, enhancing a victim stance and reinforcing a strident, ego-centered approach to life. All this is the antithesis of Vulcan's task of bringing the ego to heel. Instead, Vulcan, you should strive to use your gifts for the benefit of all, beautifying life by showing others what can be. Note well that underneath it all, Vulcan is a deeply mystical sign and that spiritual depth should be cultivated. This is your path to the greatest inner fulfillment.

Relationships with a Vulcan can be quite pleasant, or quite difficult; and often they are, by turns, both of these things. With your natural attractiveness, Vulcan, you are a wonderful companion, and your lovely words only enhance that situation. Your strong sexual desire (from Venus and Mars) adds another level to your allure. However, your judgmental style can become a burden, especially when you are feeling victimized. You can also feel disenchanted when the jewel you thought you saw as your beloved turns out to be less than valuable. Remember that "all that glitters is not gold," and your attempts to mold the other can fall flat. So, exercise the discernment gifted you by Mercury to assist you in your relationship choices.

The reverse is also true. By nature, the children of Vulcan are master illusionists, painting pretty pictures by word and appearance. It's not completely your fault, though. Like your namesake, you are a master craftsman in the area of the manipulation of appearances. You delight in it. Sometimes, though, others are not privy to that art, and can be unintentionally deceived by it. Also, don't be fooled by your own talents. See past illusion to the truth of the other and yourself. This is the best road to a good relationship. Proceed carefully in this area of life, then. Find someone who can appreciate your considerable talents, while being able to see past the superficial flash to the true jewel underneath, the real you.

Vocationally, Vulcan's greatest satisfaction can be had in areas that appeal to its natural gifts and tendencies. Careers like interior design, architecture, and jewelry appeal to the mythological side of your sign and its Martian roots, as well as to the influence of Venus. Careers like the law or criminal justice blend well with Mercury's influence (words, logical thought, planning) and fulfill Vulcan's innate desire to bring organization to the environment. And don't forget other areas, such as publishing or other forms of media, which blend Mercury's communication with the beauty and inspiration of Venus. Vulcan, you have many roads that can lead to an enriching professional life.

With your planetary influences, Vulcan, there are several body systems and areas that need your attention so that you may enjoy the best health. Areas ruled by your two Sun signs of Virgo and Libra include digestion (Virgo), as well as the kidneys and skin (Libra). Seeing to your digestive and eliminative health, therefore, is the key in staying as healthy as possible. Watch your diet carefully, as Virgo brings finicky digestion, while the influence of Mars can lead to too much digestive fire, resulting in ulcers. Pay careful attention to what your body tells you regarding which foods work and which don't. Strive to maintain good bowel health as well. To keep your Libra side happy, be sure to stay well hydrated, which will help assure that the kidneys and skin function optimally. Protect your skin from over-exposure to the sun and the ravages of blood-thirsty insects. Finally, see to your sensitive side, that is, practice good stress management. Meditation, therapeutic movement, engagement with nature, etc. will assist you in keeping your nervous system calm (Mercury), while feeding your creative side (Venus).

The symbol for the sign of Vulcan is a jewel star, signifying the artistic talents and attractive qualities of those born here. The animal associated with this star is the female tiger, and animal of immense grace, beauty, and fascination. The power of the tigress is always there, even when it is not displayed. Such is the impression those born under this star give to others.

Vulcan, you are a complex mix of energies. Attractive and clever, while prone to being fooled by your own ego, you must remain an attentive observer of your environment, both inner and outer. Appreciate your ability to influence others for good or ill. Your naturally seductive nature can bring you a great talent to impact all those you come into contact with. If you use your gifts merely for personal gain or immediate gratification, your efforts will tend to amount to nothing but transient pleasure. However, if you use them for an uplifting of yourself and others, learning to master the ego in the process, your impact will be transcendent.

You are the artist of your destiny, Vulcan. Temper yourself in the forge of spiritual development. The beautiful jewel that will arise from this process can be incomparable.

*Vulcan, unlike most of the other stars is only 9 days long.

1804 – 1875 Vulcan, Oct 11 – Oct 20
1875 – 1946 Vulcan, Oct 12 – Oct 21
1946 – 2017 Vulcan, Oct 13 – Oct 22
2017 – 2088 Vulcan, Oct 14 – Oct 23
2088 – 2159 Vulcan, Oct 15 – Oct 24
2159 – 2230 Vulcan, Oct 16 – Oct 25

Favonius
October 23 – November 5
6.40 degrees Libra to 20.00

Animal – Buffalo

Planet - Rahu

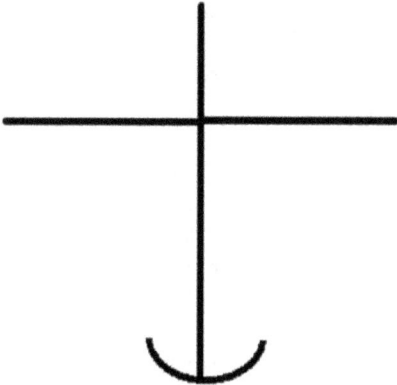

When there's a need for a compassionate soul that can talk everyone through a difficult situation, nobody has a better chance of success than you, Favonius. The term "silver-tongued" must have been invented for you. Somehow, you are able to move through complex negotiations and thorny confrontations skillfully. You were made for this.

Those born under this star possess a finely honed sense of communication and they love playing with ideas. Those of Favonius are restless learners and are quite curious. All the associations that this star has with the element of Air help to explain these qualities.

In mythology, Favonius (whose Greek name is Zephyros) is the god of the west wind. These were known to be the gentlest of breezes, heralding late spring and summer. As a result, these zephyrs were always welcome. However, Favonius wasn't a nice guy all the time. An example? Well, perhaps the best known story of him involves his being jealous of a young boy who preferred the company of Apollo to his. Once, when Apollo and the lad were playing quoits, Favonius used his windiness to divert the disc, hitting the young man in the head and killing him. In his grief, Apollo turned the young man into the hibiscus flower. So, you see, there's this jealous part to Favonius, with a generous side order of irritability.

Nevertheless, the windy, airy aspect of this sign also shows itself in a fondness for the intellect and learning. A fine ability with words, often described as "sweet," just like those gentle breezes, is also often present. What's more, Favonius lies entirely within the astrological Sun sign of Libra, which is airy by nature. Libra is ruled by Venus, a planet that gives an appreciation for beauty and its expression to those born here. Also, the star of Favonius itself is ruled by the shadowy North Node of the Moon (known as Rahu). This ruler has an essentially airy nature, while bestowing a lust for life and a desire for financial gain to those born here.

So, Favonius, this is why you have a way with words. Better still, you can also navigate the business world, having a natural savvy in this sphere, courtesy of Rahu. You are a very varied soul and boredom won't often be a problem for you. You are comfortable in settings from the boardroom to the library. In other words, there always seems to be something you are interested in. Flexibility of thought is a watchword for you, and this serves you in good times and in bad. Your approach to life is like a reed in the wind. You are able to bend with the demands of the times without breaking, while also being able to strike out in a new direction if need be.

This isn't to say that negativity can't work its way into your viewpoint. Nobody with a mind as fertile and active as yours can avoid the occasional negative space. However, since your mind is so dominant, you might sometimes tend to dwell on that negativity, to your detriment. Be very careful here, Favonius. Remember that you are also under the sign of Libra, the balance; and that is what you must strive for. By balancing an over-negative tendency with an appreciation for the positive, you can keep your mind active, agile, and content.

Like the finely tuned and sensitive balance that it is, your mind can move back and forth, restlessly trying on many ideas, and quickly changing course. This may give some people the impression that you are inconstant or fickle (which, in all honesty, can sometimes be the case). However, you'll have to be kind, Favonius. Not many can match you here. You will have to give them time to catch up. Of course, by then you may be on to something else. This can be true in other areas as well. You see, you love your independence and want to be able to shift as need be, moving like grasses in the wind. Never perfectly still, always ready to change. When others can't seem to match your pace, you might get impatient. But never let yourself lose your center, Favonius. Even the freest flowing grasses have their roots, the place from which they move. To your credit, you possess a honed intuitive sense. This may make you seem flighty; someone who goes off on irrelevant tangents. Nevertheless, you can be sure that something inside you knows, and this internal breeze is the thing guiding you.

Children of Favonius have some things to beware of as well. Yes, they have an inner compass that has proved reliable, and yes, they think and reason quickly and accurately. However, when misapplied, these gifts can lead to a self-centered approach, especially when it comes to financial pursuits. Also, that restless streak can result in a disconnected, scattered take on life. Being blown by too many winds at once only leads to confusion and wasted effort. Good advice for those of this star is always to return to center, the place of perfect balance. Often, this center revolves around the spiritual aspect of their lives. Material security is fine, but without a spiritual base, Favonius tends to suffer a deep dissatisfaction.

Vocationally, individuals born here can gain satisfaction in careers that involve communication and negotiation. The business world is a natural fit, as is the law. The financial world in the broader sense also is appealing, so financial planners and stock brokers can find a home here. The love of learning has led many children of Favonius to pursue work in academia or as librarians. The Venus influence from Libra colors everything with an artistic air, and Favonius delights in making beautiful arguments and presentations. Any area in which this can be indulged can be a source of satisfaction for the children of this star. Finally, though, the spiritual world frequently beckons. Positions with church organizations, even as priests and ministers, commonly call Favonius. Such is the complexity of these individuals. They are a seeming mix of contradictions, feeling at home in business and in the spirit. The reed can be blown in many directions by the winds of the mind.

Relationships involving a child of Favonius are always interesting, if not often settled. Keeping up with such an active mind is a challenge. Matching the sometimes quickly shifting moods is another. Yet, those of this star are kind and compassionate, willing to look at the other's position. They are well-known for their skills in negotiation and compromise, essential abilities in any successful, long-term relationship. While they can be restless and fickle at times, they are able to withstand many storms, remaining constant in difficult circumstances. In other words, once Favonius attaches, it can be tough to let go. This can lead to a sense of dependence, or worse. With a mind left to run free, jealousy can result. Intricate sets of events can be created from little evidence. Here's a tip for you, Favonius. Please check out your suppositions before you send a disc flying into someone else's head. Merely a word to the wise . . .

The key for both parties in these relationships is to honor the need for negotiation and clear communication. Favonius doesn't like to be hemmed in too much, so some room for movement is necessary. As long as they maintain their groundedness, their roots, things are more likely to work out for Favonius in a relationship.

Regarding health, Favonius needs to take care to stay in balance, especially in the eliminative organs such as the kidneys, bowels, and skin. Proper hydration is essential, as is eating foods that do not generate too much air (gas) in the digestive tract. It is very important for those of this star to be able to remain flexible, mentally and physically. Gentle, meditative movement exercise (for example, yoga, tai chi, qigong, or interpretive dance) would be of great benefit. Remember to keep yourself free to move like a gentle breeze, following your mind and changing circumstances, Favonius. However, even the most happily active mind requires some rest. For that, it would be best to spend some time in solitude, giving the mind a rest from its intense activity. Time spent in nature will yield great dividends (Libra's Venus loves natural beauty), perhaps in places where gentle breezes can caress both body and mind.

The symbol for this sign is a plant shoot rising from the ground, or an anchor (symbolizing the delving quality of the mind). The intersection of the lines shows the need for balance, and the weighing of options. The animal associated with Favonius is the buffalo. This is a sturdy animal, which is able to bear many things and "take care of business." It is a source of great strength to those born here.

Favonius, you have one of the finest minds in the zodiac. It can be put to wondrous uses, both material and spiritual. Now, sometimes you might feel unsafe until your financial security seems on solid ground. But once that hurdle is passed, it can be full speed ahead to a place of spiritual fulfillment. Then, riding the gentle breezes of the Universe will never feel better!

1804 – 1875 Favonius, Oct 21 – Nov 3
1875 – 1946 Favonius, Oct 22 – Nov 4
1946 – 2017 Favonius, Oct 23 – Nov 5
2017 – 2088 Favonius, Oct 24 – Nov 6
2088 – 2159 Favonuis, Oct 25 – Nov 7
2159 – 2230 Favonius, Oct 26 – Nov 8

Dinus
November 6 – November 18
20.00 degrees Libra to 3.20 Scorpio

Animal – Tiger

Planet - Jupiter

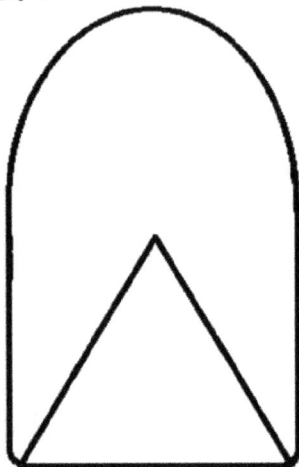

Focused. Persistent. Driven. Feel familiar to you, Dinus? These are words that you may have heard others use to describe you. Or perhaps you use them to describe yourself. It's okay; you can own these terms, because traits like these are the keys to your achievement. You are admired, sometimes even reviled, because of them. But what do you care? There's no arguing with results, is there?

You are the hard-working, will-not-be-denied member of the zodiac. Once you set your mind on something, there is little, if anything, that can dissuade you. You know that it takes time, effort, and a bit of suffering to attain anything truly worth having. And you're willing to put in the time and effort, Dinus. Pity anyone who stands in your way, too.

Dinus is a term applied to Ares, the Greek god of war (not to be confused with Aries, the zodiac sign of the ram). The name of his

Roman counterpart is Mars. The word Dinus means fearsome, and those born of this star can feel that quality surging through them, especially when roused in a cause. Like the god going to war, children of Dinus can be single-minded and fierce in their approach to a problem. Paradoxically, though, Mars was also the god of agriculture, the original "swords into plowshares" guy, one could say. In this aspect, Dinus is persistent, working long and hard until the fruits of one's labor can be harvested. The interesting interplay of the planets involved in this sign help explain these personality traits as well.

Dinus straddles the border between the astrological Sun signs of Libra (ruled by Venus) and Scorpio (ruled by Mars). The star of Dinus itself is ruled by Jupiter. The fact that Dinus is the god Mars adds an extra dash of the war deity to the mix. Without Jupiter's expansive, broad-view influence, Dinus could be bogged down in an immediate "take no prisoners" approach to life. However, the benefic giant keeps Dinus looking at the long game, bringing persistence and confidence in ultimate success. All that Mars energy provides more than enough push to see things through, while Venus humanizes the sign, lending some wit and pleasantness. After all, in mythology, Venus was the only one of the gods that could get Mars to calm down.

All of this makes for a challenging and sometimes difficult personality. Often physically strong, Dinus can be an intimidating presence. Add to this the fact that those of this star are ambitious, have goals, and are hell-bent on achieving them, come what may. Obstacles are seen as things to be run over, not negotiated around. So, Dinus, can you see why sometimes you may get the reputation for being a bit abrasive or off-putting? Agreed, you can be very affable, but that tends to be when things are going your way. Honestly, how long does that affability last when you become frustrated? Of course, you are competent. You seldom attempt things without being assured that you can succeed. Why waste the effort otherwise? Oh, you can take some delay. You know that it's the long term that counts. If your way of doing things was compared to the fable of the ant and the grasshopper, you would be the ant for sure, but on steroids. You can burn very hot when you need to, Mars coupled with Jupiter's enthusiasm makes sure of that;

but you can also smolder, keeping the fire low and persistent, knowing that this steadiness will bring you that which you seek.

It's not only in actions that Dinus applies its talents, either. Children of Dinus are born debaters, with Libra's Venus giving them a desire for exactitude in words. Dinus often takes issue with every point, arguing it with the persistence for which this sign is known. No slippery logic or half-thought-out opinion can escape the magnifying glass (some might say nitpicking) scrutiny of this sign. Opinionated and forceful, those of this sign want to know why, because they will not build a house upon sand. They are planners, methodical and measured, but they can also surge ahead when the moment is right. They are firm believers in striking when the iron (the metal sacred to Mars) is hot.

Dinus, you are a powerhouse, without a doubt. But it comes at a cost. It is paramount for you to learn to watch your frustration level. When roused, you can become aggressive and dictatorial. Mars simply gets out of control. At such times, you can be overly pushy in your agenda, alienating even those that want to help you. It's tough to want to get behind a quarrelsome nitpicker, you know. You run the real risk of isolating yourself, and as John Donne famously said, "No man is an island." Not even you, Dinus. Of course, the opposite can be the case. With your considerable drive and energy, you may take on too much, as an unruly Jupiter scatters your efforts. It's not an easy line to walk, but, given careful attention, you can do it. Ultimately, the nurturing of patience is the key; and you know you can be patient. You are the cultivator of results. You take ideas and incubate them, planfully gestating them until they are ready to bear fruit. So when Mars starts to run amok, remember that at your core you can be a master strategist. Sometimes a controlled burn is called for, at other times a wildfire. Knowing when each is appropriate will bring you the best outcomes.

A relationship with a child of Dinus can be a rocky ride. Flashes of excitement are tempered by quiet, persistent devotion to a goal. There are times when Dinus seems to leave the other out of the equation entirely, especially when focused on the latest project. On the other hand, those of this star often have a strong sex appetite (all that Mars with a dash of Venus), and look for such attention frequently. When too often denied, Dinus can become bitter, resentful, and even jealous. The results can be fireworks-filled disagreements. At times, Dinus may even initiate extra-relational affairs. This temptation toward infidelity has been the death knell of many relationships involving the children of Mars. What is required for Dinus is to marshal that famous perseverance and turn it toward nurturing the relationship. Using the forces of Venus and Jupiter, a greater sense of selflessness can be cultivated, moving the Mars energy more toward plowshares than swords. If you truly value a relationship, Dinus, what better project to nurture, what better goal to set you sights on, than that?

When it comes to vocation, anything that involves the strengths of this sign would bring fulfillment. Careers that require meticulous planning and sustained effort call for the talents that Dinus brings. Research, from the lab to the world of journalism, is a promising avenue. With all that Mars energy, careers in the military or law enforcement, with the gradual advancement inherent in those arenas, would be a good fit for many born under this star. Politics and the law can also beckon. Needless to say, those born of Dinus may chafe in a situation where personal initiative is not rewarded, or where their plans are frequently thwarted.

High energy, hard-driving Dinus has a couple of areas where health may be of concern. These are linked directly to the Sun signs under which Dinus falls. Libra reminds Dinus to attend to body systems concerned with excretion, such as the kidneys and bowels. Scorpio warns to be aware of reproductive health. Keep a watchful eye for problems with the prostate in males, or ovaries and uterus in females. Infertility may be an issue as well. The heat from all that Mars energy can also lead to problems in the stomach. Food choices should be made so that stomach upset is avoided. Perhaps the most important thing for Dinus to cultivate is a sense of calm. Learning to deal with stress and frustration is paramount for anyone born here. The force and heat of a Dinus personality, when turned against the self, can wreak havoc physically, mentally, and emotionally. Cultivating a spiritual practice can accomplish several goals by modulating physical reactions, calming thoughts, and tempering emotions. Of course, the spiritual growth that results is an added bonus.

The symbol for this sign is a triumphal gateway, signifying the attainment of a goal and martial success. Note, however, that it also somewhat suggests a peace sign. Swords and plowshares. The animal associated with this sign is (what else?) the tiger. Magnificent and fearsome, carefully stalking its prey and choosing the exact moment to strike, the tiger reminds Dinus to direct its force patiently, and in the best way to achieve long-term success.

When your talents and energy are properly channeled, you are truly a force to be reckoned with, Dinus. You have the ability to maintain for the long haul like no other sign. You can be irascible, and you will have to learn to master that tendency, turning it toward the achievement of your goals. You have lessons to teach the rest of humanity, lessons of perseverance and confidence of eventual success. It will take time, you know that; but taking time is something at which you excel.

1804 – 1875 Dinus, Nov 4 – Nov 16
1875 – 1946 Dinus, Nov 5 – Nov 17
1946 – 2017 Dinus, Nov 6 – Nov 18
2017 – 2088 Dinus, Nov 7 – Nov 19
2088 – 2159 Dinus, Nov 8 – Nov 20
2159 – 2230 Dinus, Nov 9 – Nov 21

Urania
November 19 – December 1
3.20 degrees Scorpio to 16.40

Animal – Rabbit

Planet - Saturn

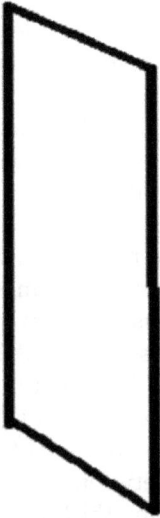

You've never had much trouble getting along with people, have you, Urania? You're the one that everyone just seems to like, even if they don't know why. Regardless of whether you are a social butterfly or not, there's something about you that others recognize. It's the feeling that you are a person who can meet someone else right where they are.

Urania is one of the titles applied to Venus (Aphrodite in Greek). The word means heavenly or spiritual. This title was used to distinguish the pure, celestial love quality of Venus from the more material, carnal, and lustful aspect of the goddess of love. In this guise, Venus is at her spiritual best, a love that expresses as transcendent beauty. Here she is the abstraction of generative powers, as opposed to the sexual act itself. This becomes, for those born under this star, a mystical, deep knowing and an appreciation for the wonder of all of creation. A curious mix of planetary forces is at work here as well.

Urania is entirely contained within the astrological Sun sign of Scorpio, ruled by Mars. The star itself is ruled by Saturn, the planet of limitation. Finally, the star's name indicates that Venus is a potent force here as well. So, composing this star are action (Mars), challenge (Saturn), and heavenly beauty (Venus). Quite the mix! However, these forces blend together very well. Venus in her aspect as Urania is abstract, unrestricted beauty, which needs some form (limits, Saturn's function) placed upon it in order to manifest in the real world. Once manifested, it requires energy or force (Mars) to take action. From this interaction, the children of Urania display their qualities.

There is a natural attractiveness to you, Urania, and people usually like you, or at least don't dislike you. Part of this fascination comes from Scorpio, whose residents tend to exude a mysterious, mystical quality. In Urania, the natural bellicose quality of Mars is tempered by the loving, compassionate Venus, resulting in individuals who are usually loyal and loving. Others often look to you for organizational skill and leadership qualities, too. Your ability to get along with many types of people makes you naturally facile at being a go-between, the glue of the group. Children of Urania are interested in many things, allowing them to converse or consult in a number of areas. You love variety, Urania, and this can manifest as a restless mind or body. That is, you love to travel, whether mentally, in your thoughts, or physically, in foreign lands. With this in-born ability to get along, you can find fulfillment at home or around the world.

As someone born under Urania, one of your great lessons is to learn to balance the various aspects of your life. This is also evident in the pull of the planetary energies at work within you. A real, inner struggle goes on occasionally. You possess the fullness of beauty that is the abstract Venus, which chafes now and again against the limits of weighty Saturn. Meanwhile, Mars is the energetic bridge, powering the show. It can be a regular three ring circus inside you sometimes! Here is your challenge then. You must come to terms with the fact that success in the business world, for instance, must not be at the cost of your relationships and friendships, or vice versa. Urania can easily feel pulled in opposite directions. The trick is balance.

This balance is often hard-won. Venus bestows a desire to create, to give birth. Many times Urania's children feel the desire to go off in new directions, wherever their wandering minds or bodies take them. Not infrequently, this can lead to a starving of close relationships if not handled carefully. This desire to explore and expand their horizons can be reinforced by hardships when young. Urania, you often experience some form of deprivation when a child, either physical or emotional. Sometimes there is a lack of nurturance by the mother (the generative Venus of one's youth). These circumstances can stimulate in you a desire for more, all while tending to your interpersonal relationships in a way that assures growth. The scars of this early deprivation can remain in you. Usually, they take the form of persistent melancholy, moodiness, or a secretive nature. Fortunately for you, Urania, you commonly possess empathic or psychic talents, helping you to understand the deeper aspects of human interaction.

An area where Urania tends to shine is in relationships, as they are capable of honoring both themselves and the other fully. Those born under this star are generally loving, loyal, kind, and devoted to those close to them. In fact, they are faithful almost to a fault, sometimes being taken advantage of by others as a result. They are staunch defenders of those they care about, and are cooperative in their approach. This lends itself well to the ordinary give and take of a well-functioning relationship. As long as they are not given reason to be jealous, relationships are rewarding and fulfilling for both parties. However, when jealous, Urania, you can be angry, even cruel. This is when the combined forces of Mars and Saturn arise to create conflict and discord. Now, Urania will deny this tendency vigorously, but there's no getting around it. This is your dark side when it comes to relationships. In fact, it is a common temptation for Urania to become quite passive-aggressive at such times; smiling to someone's face while stabbing them in the back. So keep your eyes open to those times,

Urania, and see if you can send a little, loving Venus through to the situation.

The anger issues (Mars and Saturn) mentioned above are the primary negative aspect of the Urania personality. You can have residual anger from childhood adversity. This anger can spew out in any direction, particularly when the wrong you feel reminds you of difficulties from your younger years. There may also be a tendency to be over-controlling of others. It is very important, Urania, to be sure to manage that anger, look at it, and see if it is justified. Anger problems can be especially problematic when those born here harness any psychic or occult gifts for ill ends. Nothing but trouble lies in this direction, Urania. Misuse of these abilities generates problems for all concerned, you included. It is best to learn to deal with anger and frustration in a constructive fashion. Sowing forgiveness lets Venus shine through and redirects the other planetary energies to manifest a better environment so that healing can occur.

Given their ability to get along with almost anyone, while also being natural organizers, children of Urania shine in business settings. Anywhere that cooperation is necessary fits their personality well, as they can focus on a goal, while also being ready to share in a common endeavor. Diligent workers, those born here are often excellent managers and planners. And don't forget the travel bug, either. Urania, you can find satisfaction anywhere in the travel industry, as it appeals to your insatiable desire for variety. That certainly includes internal travel as well. Urania natives can be wonderful guides for inner exploration, for example, as interpreters of dreams. Finally, given the strong Scorpio component, careers that deal with the depths of anything are also promising, as Scorpio is known for delving into the darkest crannies of anything. From this perspective, possibilities include mining (or any vocation that involves digging), dentistry, even plumbing!

Children of Urania are usually blessed with a good level of vitality and live long lives. However, they need to be aware of a couple of issues. Digestion can be tricky, and Urania should keep an eye on the stomach and the colon. It is important for Urania's children to keep their bowels regular and to maintain a steady diet, as they are prone to suffer when meals are irregular. Proper hydration is an absolute must to keep the entire system well lubricated. Additionally, in women, there may be menstrual irregularities. Also, Urania, be sure to keep your immune system functioning at its best, as you may be more prone to colds and sore throats. Importantly, don't let your anger eat you up on the inside. Fortunately, Urania's offspring are often natural mystics, and those born here can usually connect with the realm of spirit fairly easily. Therefore, by all means cultivate a relaxation or meditation practice. Well thought out affirmations wouldn't hurt, either. Pay attention to these suggestions, and you will grace the world with your presence for a long time.

The symbol for Urania is a staff, symbolic of this signs propensity for travel of all kinds, as well as its ability to triumph over adversity. The animal of Urania is the rabbit, a creature that travels quickly, but is gentle and nurturing. It is also a symbol of fertility, a reminder of the association of this sign with Venus.

Urania, you show the way toward cooperation while holding your own center. You can be mysterious and inviting, showing others both compassion and direction. Your biggest challenge is learning to balance the important aspects of your life so than no one area dominates. Accomplish this, and you will be the embodiment of the celestial Venus, who loves and inspires all.

1804 – 1875 Urania, Nov 17 – Nov 29
1875 – 1946 Urania, Nov 18 – Nov 30
1946 – 2017 Urania, Nov 19 – Dec 1
2017 – 2088 Urania, Nov 20 – Dec 2
2088 – 2159 Urania, Nov 21 – Dec 3
2159 – 2230 Urania, Nov 22 – Dec 4

Parca

December 2 – December 14
16.40 degrees Scorpio to 30.00

Animal – Rabbit

Planet - Mercury

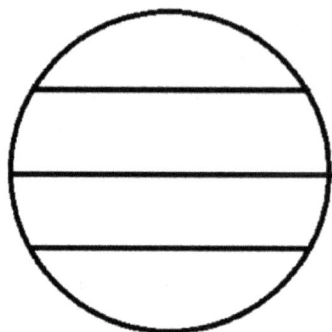

People look to you, Parca. You know they do, and sometimes you might wonder why. What might they expect? It seems as if they think you hold some deep wisdom, some inner power – and you do, even if you don't realize it. This is both the promise and the challenge of your star.

You see, Parca is the name that was applied to the Fates in mythology. At each person's birth, the Fates would spin the thread of that individual's life, destining them for all the good or ill that would befall them. They were independent of any other force and so powerful that even the gods had to submit to their determination. Starting to see why people regard you the way that they do? That force of deep knowledge resides in those born here, and it can bring great power to Parca's children.

The sign of Parca lies entirely within the sign of Scorpio, extending to the very end of this Mars-ruled Sun sign. Parca lies in the heart of Scorpio, and includes the red supergiant star Antares, whose name literally means a rival or competitor of Mars (anti-Ares, the Greek name for the god of war). This gigantic star is so named because it has often been confused with the red planet in the sky, due to their similar color (Curiously, the diameter of the body of this star is just a bit larger than that of Mars's orbit around the Sun). At any rate, Parca, you have a large dose of Martian energy from Antares and Scorpio's planetary ruler. Completing the mix is Mercury, the planet that rules Parca itself. This is the planet of mental agility and worldly knowledge. All these combine to give you the aura of a person of wisdom who knows when and how to take action.

It could be said that there is no typical Parca, so different are these people in their outward dealings with the world. However, at their core, there is always that sense of inner knowing mentioned above. Children of Parca are often seen as elders somehow, even when they aren't. For instance, a Parca could be the youngest child in a family, yet this individual is looked to in a way that one might look to the eldest, for guidance. Precisely how this tendency shows depends on the particular life circumstances of the person.

At their best, those born here are caring and charitable, deliberate and kind. They will readily take on responsibility, and bear up admirably under it. Their accomplishments tend to be earned through their own hard work. Parcas wear a sense of seniority or superiority well, becoming a protective leader of those entrusted to them. Many people of great power are born here, and courage is one of their finest assets.

There is an entirely different story of Parca at its worst, however. In this case, the responsibilities that have been shouldered lead to resentment, irritability, and criticism. The usual self-esteem of Parca is rational and good. But when Parca feels put upon, or feels victimized by responsibility and the expectations of others, there is a stark decline in their self-assessment. Parca in a negative space is highly self-critical, and can become secretive. Not very attractive, Parca. At times like these, you can harbor a simmering anger, even lashing out against others in a cruel and insensitive fashion.

For sure, others perceive Parca as having the wisdom of the elders. The resulting pressure put upon Parca by others can lead to wildly fluctuating levels of security in those born here. For example, they can suffer from financial ups and downs, trouble in relationships, and changing moods. This situation is made more intense by the fact that Parca's children know at some level that they have this inner wisdom, too. As such, they can come to expect quite a lot of themselves, and can feel acute disappointment when they do not measure up to their self-imposed standards. This can lead to withdrawal, in an attempt to avoid facing that disappointment head-on.

Parca, you know that you have many gifts, and if you feel that you are not fully utilizing them, it can be very upsetting. You are aware that you possess a fine mind (Mercury) that is powered by a drive to action (Mars). This gives you a calculated ability to take charge, plan, and daringly undertake any task set before you. What's more, your heart is easily touched by the plight of others, making you quite generous with your time or resources. Usually, however, you are not flashy, and carry your inner authority with quiet grace. This can make you seem dull to others; yet there is always something going on behind your seemingly bland exterior. You know that you will be there when needed, reliable and steady.

In relationships, Parcas are as varied as they are in other areas of their lives. Generally, Parca can be expected to take on responsibility and be in a position to offer advice and guidance, which makes them good helpmates. It's how they react to this situation that spells the difference. As long as it's not seen as a burden, and their input is valued, Parca's natural tendency toward charity and protectiveness will function positively. If not, be prepared for resentment and condescension. Parca, it's so important for you to feel that you are seen as a positive force in a relationship, both by you and by the other. Under these conditions, your beneficent power will blossom, nurturing the relationship. But if you don't "feel the love," you will be sorely tempted to become secretive, angry, and arrogant. Your need for control will go into high gear, making the relationship a chore for you, and an unbearable situation for the other. To counter this, be sure to keep the lines of communication open at all times. Be willing to take suggestions and allow compromise. Finally, don't get consumed by worry. If you maintain this stance, your judgment will often be deferred to, allowing you to feel comfortable and magnanimous. The relationship will grow as a result.

No doubt about it, Parca, you need to learn to control the thornier parts of your personality. When you feel bad about yourself, it is too easy for your ego to slip beyond your control, bringing out a tendency toward pride, irritability, and argumentativeness. In order for you to progress spiritually, and to be truly happy, bad feelings must not be allowed to dominate your view of life. You hold a powerful key within you. Trust in that inner knowing to bring you the greatest sense of fulfillment.

In the work world, Parca can find satisfaction in a number of areas. Those born here do have good executive ability, so management positions suit them well, as does any form of self-employment. Parca, you don't do as well under someone's thumb, or in positions where you are not in a position to make decisions that directly affect the outcome of a project. Your often quiet sense of authority will speak more loudly than empty commands. Also, you can think great thoughts (thank you, Mercury), so positions in higher education may feel comfortable. All that Mars energy could attract you to a career in the military or law enforcement. Coupled with your innate leadership abilities, such hierarchical situations can be a great fit. Take charge, Parca. You were meant for it. However, in any career, it is important that you feel respected and rewarded. You have a real desire for prosperity, too. When that desire is taken care of, you are free to grow in other dimensions of your being, while keeping the bugaboo of low self-esteem at bay.

Regarding health, Parca must be especially aware of areas that respond to the energies of Mars and Scorpio, like the genitals, muscles, and head. While vigorous exercise appeals to the Mars in you, be careful to warm up properly to prevent muscle injuries. The heat of Mars can affect digestion, so be sure not to over-indulge in spicy foods, or anything that will aversely influence the bowels (ruled by Scorpio). The Mercury rulership of Parca can also bring tension headaches or nervous irritability. In fact, stress breaks are important, especially since so many people count on you so often. You need to get away from it all for a bit, for your own good. Gentle motion exercises like yoga or tai chi can help, as can walks in nature, even in open fields, which can calm the energy of Mars.

The symbol for Parca is a round amulet, pendant, or earring, indicating authority and a high position. Such adornments have historically been worn by government officials as a symbol of office and power. Parca, let this symbol remind you of the abilities that lie within you. The animal associated with this sign is the rabbit, a creature of great creativity (the generativity of Scorpio). The rabbit totem has also been used by shamans to give wisdom, awareness, and intuition – three qualities of Parca.

You were born to bring wisdom and leadership to humanity, Parca. You might not be flashy, but your quiet command draws attention and respect nonetheless. It is often up to you to take charge. Don't fear that responsibility. Use your inner resources to show the way. Then, you can become the master of your own fate. It is your birthright!

1804 – 1875 Parca, Nov 30 – Dec 12
1875 – 1946 Parca, Dec 1 – Dec 13
1946 – 2017 Parca, Dec 2 – Dec 14
2017 – 2088 Parca, Dec 3 – Dec 15
2088 – 2159 Parca, Dec 4 – Dec 16
2159 – 2230 Parca, Dec 5 – Dec 17

Hecate
December 15 – December 27
00.0 degrees Sag to 13.20

Animal – Dog

Planet - Ketu

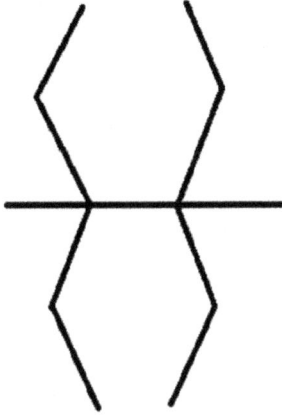

What are you researching today, Hecate? What bit of knowledge, what mystery are you trying to get to the root of? You know that you are always investigating, pondering, and wondering. Truth with a capital T – that's your aim, and finding it is your gift.

In mythology, Hecate is the goddess of magic, witchcraft, and the night. As such, she is also commonly associated with the Moon. This goddess endeavors to bring light to the dark areas and to work with hidden forces to effect change. For instance, Hecate guided Persephone through the darkness on her trip to the underworld. In fact, in art Hecate is often depicted holding twin torches, illuminating that which was once unknown. The combination of planetary forces at work here supports this function perfectly.

This star lies wholly within the astrological Sun sign of Sagittarius the centaur, ruled by Jupiter. Hecate itself is ruled by the Moon's south node, Ketu. The association of Hecate with the Moon gives some emphasis to the lunar power contained within those born here as well. Jupiter lends an expansive quality, one which keeps Hecate's children exploring and researching. The double lunar influence (from Ketu and Hecate's identification as a Moon goddess) brings a comfort with the dark, the unseen, and the hidden. What this means, Hecate, is that you can see through the darkness, finding your way even in the midst of the most confusing circumstances. This is what makes you such a gifted researcher and seeker after truth.

Without a doubt, the most enduring quality of the children of Hecate is the ability to dig to the root of things. Associated with witchcraft, one of Hecate's powers lies with plant medicine, and you may find yourself drawn to studying herbalism or gardening in general. This parallels the everyday urge to get to the root of any issue confronting you. Meanwhile, you are not afraid to get your hands dirty when searching for the truth lying at the base of a situation. You aren't easily deterred, either.

Those born of Hecate are ambitious and persistent, with your natural inquisitiveness driving you onward. Unafraid of hard work, you soldier on despite setbacks or obstacles. Blockages to your progress are often met with a head-on attack, or by the application of your innate shrewdness and cleverness. Many of Hecate's children taste the fruits of their labor in the form of luxury and material riches, an added bonus to the discovery of the truth that you so doggedly pursue.

Ah, but Hecate both gives and takes away. That is her nature, and her children often experience the results of this trait of the dark goddess. It is not uncommon for those born here to suffer sudden and extreme reversals, or to be saddled with financial or other environmental burdens. Life's circumstances can indeed feel stifling to Hecate's children, as if they were lost in the darkness, deprived of the light of their goddess's torch. When so trapped, resentment commonly surfaces, as does a feeling of being betrayed by life.

Also, this sign's having Ketu as a planetary ruler doesn't make matters any easier. Ketu tends to be less concerned with the material world, and everyday disappointments are in keeping with its uneven attention to this realm. Ketu asks that those born here look beyond the physical when under adverse circumstances, and to see the spiritual lesson that lies beneath. In other words, Hecate, turn your natural investigative powers inward. Apply them to your own spirit, as opposed to some external quest. Even when things seem dark and bleak, you can muster the light to make sense of it all.

However, when things get the better of Hecate, the shadow side of this sign can certainly arise. Here is found the arrogance, ego, and anger of someone who expects to be rewarded materially for all of the hard work they have done. When Hecate feels unjustly treated by reversals of fortune, these negative traits can easily come to the surface. Growing spiteful and bitter, Hecate can lose sight of the bigger picture, and fall into a deep depression. Remember, Hecate, the lesson is always spiritual. Search for that lesson in order to make sense of, or at least accept, the tough times.

Relationships with those of this sign can be fascinating and challenging, or dark and exasperating. The desire to reach the truth brings a direct and uplifting aspect to relationships. There is a strong, philosophical side to Hecate, which lends a taste for deep conversation and thoughtful consideration of issues. Don't expect to get away with facile answers when in a relationship with Hecate. The desire is always to root out the truth and to gain an ultimate understanding of any issue. Be prepared for long, sometimes exhaustive and far-ranging discussions. Anyone in a relationship with Hecate will see their horizons broadened as they race along with the centaur in the pursuit of the Answer. But that's not to say that Hecate is all abstract thought. Children of this star can be subject to expansive emotions and passionate pursuits, thanks to fiery Sagittarius and its ruler Jupiter. The dark and mysterious lunar side of Hecate's nature can keep things interesting and a bit unpredictable as well.

Just be sure to keep the negative aspects of your personality in check, Hecate, to gain success in relationships. You can be subject to some of the greatest reversals of fortune of all the zodiac stars. Here will be the greatest test of your inner strength, as well as your ability to navigate the ups and downs of any relationship. Let ego and arrogance seize control, and you stand the risk of destroying even a good relationship.

Part of Hecate's function is to dissolve old structures so that new ones can form. It is an inherent part of her wisdom that suffering in this life is inevitable, but the amount of physical or emotional pain that accompanies it is variable. This suffering merely serves the purpose of putting things onto the right track. In relationships, it can mean growth and enrichment, but only if it's handled carefully and in the proper manner. One thing is for sure, though. Anyone in a relationship with you, Hecate, is in for an interesting ride!

In the realm of career, Hecate shines in any field that involves research and investigation. Scientific and medical fields lend themselves to this, especially areas that involve chemical or plant-based (e.g., pharmaceutical or herbal) pursuits. In particular, specialties that look at pain and consciousness can be appealing (the light of awareness versus the dark of unconsciousness or sleep – remember Hecate and Persephone). The classic association of Hecate with herbalism could lead to a vocation in this area, or even a simple interest in plants and growing things. Additionally, there might be a pull toward investigation in the form of detective work or as a lawyer. While the philosophical, truth-seeking side of Hecate would feel very much at home in an academic setting, a natural fit might also be in the area of religion and the realm of the spirit. There is a powerful, spiritual urge in you, Hecate, and this can come out in writing, speaking, or teaching about a religious or spiritual path. Don't forget Hecate's rulership of magic, and Ketu's emphasis on the mystical when thinking about a vocation. Professions like astrology or the study of other arcane sciences would certainly fit the energies of this star. As long as the desire to seek after truth or to get to the root of the matter is present, Hecate can find satisfaction in a career.

Those born under this star have particular health concerns in line with the attributes of its Sun sign. Sagittarius rules the hips and thighs, so Hecate should be aware of problems in the structure of these areas, including the sciatic nerve. Proper exercise, including walking and practices that stretch the hips and legs, such as tai chi or yoga, would be beneficial. Too much of an inner orientation, bringing about physical inertia from too much thought, can lead to weight problems. Hecate remains sharpest when feeling physically nimble, so temper proper diet with appropriate exercise. Meditation can also help disperse the over-accumulation of left brain, thought-centered energy, bringing stress relief and a more open mental viewpoint. These inner practices can also help to banish the moodiness and darkness of mien that haunt a Hecate under stress. Finally, be aware of liver concerns. The liver is the body's chemical factory and detoxification facility, fitting in with Hecate's emphasis on herbal medicine. Natural and regular liver cleansing can prove to be a useful avenue if liver concerns arise.

The symbol for Hecate resembles a bundle of roots, symbolizing the primary drive of those born here. These roots are bound at the center point, the place of ultimate truth. The animal associated with this sign is the dog, an animal that sniffs out the cause of things, while pursuing its quarry unrelentingly. This totem calls to mind the "dogged" fashion in which Hecate follows the path to the truth.

Without you, Hecate, truth would lose one of its staunchest allies. You broach no slipshod or half-hearted attempts to come to grips with the base of what is. Your ambition is an inspiration, and at your best you unite the mental and the spiritual in a powerful combination. It's up to you, Hecate, to light the way in the darkness!

1804 – 1875 Hecate, Dec 13 – Dec 25
1875 – 1946 Hecate, Dec 14 – Dec 26
1946 – 2017 Hecate, Dec 15 – Dec 27
2017 – 2088 Hecate, Dec 16 – Dec 28
2088 – 2159 Hecate, Dec 17 – Dec 29
2159 – 2230 Hecate, Dec 18 – Dec 30

Ceto
December 28 – January 9
13.20 degrees Sag to 26.40

Animal – Monkey

Planet - Venus

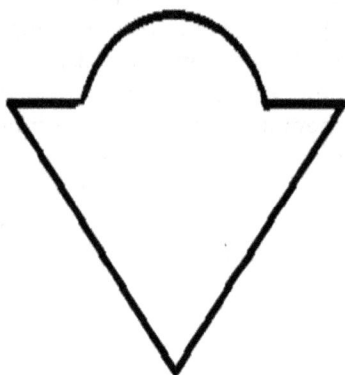

Excelsior! That should be your watchword, Ceto. You are always looking for a new challenge or something new to accomplish. It can be tough to keep up with you. Not many can. Even fewer try.

You were born under a star named for the marine goddess who ruled over the dangers of the sea. Her particular creatures were large mammals, like whales and dolphins (creatures we call cetaceans today, in honor of her). Also in her province were the scary denizens of the deep, including the various sea monsters of myth and legend. To top it off, she was also mother of the gorgons, those delightful creatures that included Medusa. While all this sounds pretty foreboding, those born here often enjoy a great deal of popularity. The planetary energies at play here help to explain this.

Ceto lies entirely within the astrological Sun sign of Sagittarius, whose ruling planet is Jupiter. The sign of Ceto itself is ruled by lovely and charming Venus. Both of these planets are considered good planets, or benefics, in astrology. The section of the constellation of Sagittarius covered by Ceto includes the centaur's bow, which also bears a resemblance to a fan or shell. In the personality of the children of Ceto, Jupiter lends an expansive, likeable quality, while Venus (who arose from the sea on a shell, according to some tales) adds physical appeal. The fan implies popularity, elegance, and a bit of mystery too. All in all, Ceto enjoys a reputation as someone everybody would like to know, or at least say that they know.

Those born under Ceto are strivers who look constantly for ways to improve themselves. They wish to take things and make them purer, sleeker, and more refined. What's even more, they tend to make it look easy. In fact, they can seem invincible. No challenge is too great, no task too formidable. They have a commanding presence and an independent streak. They are a proud breed, and seem to have an innate ability to influence great numbers of people while giving each person a feel of personal contact. Everybody wants to hang with you, Ceto!

Most people, however, don't know your inner side. You possess a philosophical and emotional depth. They don't realize that you are driven to achieve, almost obsessively so. They may not see your inner focus and how it drives you ever onward. Others don't understand the pain and confusion you endure when you are confused; how you can lose your focus and become almost passive, so very un-Ceto. They also may not see your dark side, unless you are pushed to your limit.

You do have a dark side, Ceto, and it's not very pretty at all. When your trigger is tripped, you can exhibit the fierceness of your patron goddess and her offspring. At these times, you can become aggressive and angry. You adopt a strongly confrontational style, and the great person everyone wants to be with disappears. What replace it are the gorgon and the sea monster, harsh creatures that are terrible to encounter. Fortunately for all concerned, this doesn't happen all that often. But when it does, it brings you the risk of disgrace, and you could wind up being shunned by the very crowd that fawned over you before.

Generally, though, the children of Ceto serve as an inspiration and a beacon to follow. They have plenty of energy, and are invigorated and invigorating. Fame can come easily to them, and it spreads just as easily. The down side of this, however, is that it can turn a Ceto's head. Your biggest enemy is your own ego, Ceto. You might just start believing all that stuff people are whispering in your ear. When that happens, Jupiter's energy gets out of control and you can become over-bearing and inconsiderate. Hubris comes to the fore. Then, those that challenge you have a good chance of being brought down, either by your temper or by your superior argumentative style.

You know you are a good debater, with the lovely phrasing of Venus complemented by the broad, strong style of Jupiter. You express your opinions well, but be warned, Ceto. Listening is an important skill, too. Don't be so obstinate in your position that you can't hear potentially helpful feedback. You can afford to be magnanimous, since you are able to accomplish so much and meet challenges so easily. Nevertheless, a little input form others might be just the ticket sometimes.

What has been mentioned above is never so true as when it comes to relationships. Ceto values independence, and is not comfortable with someone who doesn't feel the same. Yet, this star also enjoys the recognition of others. Such a tricky balance can be maintained, but it requires some negotiation. You need to accomplish, Ceto, and you don't want anyone to hold you back. Your partner must be comfortable to be with someone who is sought after and looked up to. At the same time, you cannot subjugate your partner beneath your own ego needs. If your dark side begins to dominate the picture, you can say good-bye to any relationship worth having – and you know that's true. Having a partner that can provide you with a challenge and inspire you to reach higher is just the ticket for you. With your charisma and charm, you can afford to be picky. As a result, it is best to wait until the right person comes along. Don't forget, though, that you aren't the only one in the relationship. Honoring the other is an important part of your life's lesson. You must be able to subjugate your ego, and devote yourself to something besides your own advancement. When that happens, the relationship can become a spiritual path, inspiring you to accomplish a great deal in an entirely new realm.

Ceto's knack for accomplishment can serve in a wide variety of careers. The persuasive speaking skills that the children of Ceto possess can bring satisfaction in fields such as writing and teaching. Vocations that rely on debate skills, such as politics and the law, are also promising. The natural appeal of natives of this sign also serves well in fields like acting or public speaking. Ceto is a natural at making connections and leaving a good impression. These are obviously desirable qualities to have in business or social networking. Any field in which connecting with others is essential may be quite attractive to Ceto. Finally, don't forget that Venus rules this sign, and Ceto is at home in the sea. Put these together, and careers that involve the sea, such as shipping and boating, would be a natural fit for those born here. Whatever field you pick, Ceto, be sure that there is room for advancement and real challenges to be met. Your inner drives will be satisfied with nothing less.

In the realm of health, Ceto faces challenges that parallel the ruling powers of the sign. Sagittarius rules the hips and legs, so care needs to be taken with these areas of the body, especially regarding their structure. This also includes the nerves of the low back and legs, like the sciatic nerve. With all the water emphasis of this sign, the bladder and kidney are also areas of concern. Be sure to stay well hydrated, maintain a proper diet, and exercise those hips and legs! Walking, running, and, in particular, swimming would fit well with Ceto's talents and tendencies. A bit of competition can keep Ceto's interest, since this star is always looking to accomplish and achieve. Even beating your own best time will keep things popping for you. Misuse of the Venus energy can result in sexually transmitted diseases, so be sure to take proper precautions. Also, meditation will calm that dark side energy of your, Ceto. It is a practice that comes highly advised.

The symbol for this sign combines a stylized shell, recalling both Ceto the water goddess and Venus's preferred vehicle for sea travel. It also suggests the fan, symbol of Ceto and the shape of this sign's asterism.

The animal associated with this sign is the monkey, a creature that climbs high, is energetic, but one that can be set off unpredictably, putting on large, loud displays of anger.

Ceto, you have been given the ability to achieve greatness. Noting seems too daunting for your lofty drives. You are an inspiration to many, and when at your best you can lift many people up to a higher place. If you can master your ego, purifying its dark side, and see to your spiritual advancement, you will truly achieve the highest of all goals.

1804 – 1875 Ceto, Dec 26 – Jan 7
1875 – 1946 Ceto, Dec 27 – Jan 8
1946 – 2017 Ceto, Dec 28 – Jan 9
2017 – 2088 Ceto, Dec 29 – Jan 10
2088 – 2159 Ceto, Dec 30 – Jan 11
2159 – 2230 Ceto, Dec 31 – Jan 12

Natura

January 10 – January 22
26.40 degrees Sag to 10.00 Cap

Animal – Mongoose

Planet - Sun

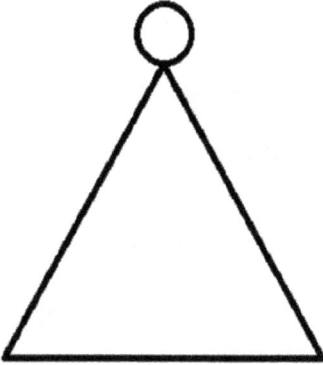

When people talk about you, Natura (and you know that they do), one word keeps coming up over and over again. That word is "intense." You do create an impression, even if it's not always the best kind. The sheer force of your personality ensures that you are not easily forgotten.

Born during this time, you embody the powers of Nature itself. Your star is named for the primeval goddess of nature, one of the first worshipped by humanity. This goddess encompassed the nature world in all its beauty, mystery, majesty, and variability. So it is with those born under this star. They are a variable group for sure, so much so that describing the typical child of Natura is a challenge. Nevertheless, there are some qualities that shine through in all those born here. The planetary energies involved help to pin this down a bit.

Natura lies within two astrological Sun signs, the latter part of Sagittarius and the beginning of Capricorn. These signs are ruled by the planets Jupiter and Saturn, respectively. Natura itself is ruled by the Sun. So, let's take a look, shall we? Jupiter: expansive, fortunate, beneficent but capricious – check. Saturn: focused, worldly, practical –

check. Sun: regal, leader, fiery – check. Blend these energies together and what results is a personality that is certainly confident and engaging, able to focus on a task single-mindedly, while having enough luck to find success. Often, the children of Natura take an interest in the plight of their fellow humans, and seek to make a positive change in the world. In this as in all matters, Natura, you usually accomplish exactly what you set out to do. You make a strong impression with your perseverance. Others see you as devoted to a set of principles that you uphold wholeheartedly, and even describe you as virtuous sometimes. Not afraid to take a stand when you feel it necessary, you can be rather controversial. But admit it. Part of you loves the attention.

The many moods of Natura are yet another matter to consider. Those born here are as variable in their mood as the changing weather. One minute, they can be as calm and soothing as a late spring day, while becoming a raging hurricane the next. This can be disconcerting to those around you, Natura. Especially those close to you. Sometimes, even your friends and family will lovingly describe you as "bonkers," while those not as kindly disposed to you will use less complimentary terms. This can make you hard to be around, particularly when you get into the whole "intensity" thing. As tough as it might be for you, a little dose of lighten-up can go a long way.

When you set your sights on something, you display a dogged determination matched by few others. You usually have abundant energy, and this stamina serves you well in any quest or challenge set before you. Keeping at something despite frustration and setbacks is a real strength for you, and it's a good thing, too. Children of Natura don't often score right out of the box, but need to stick with their goals for a long time. Blame Saturn, planet of delays, if you will, but remember that Saturn also gives you the will and determination to carry on. Meanwhile, your Jupiter side is ever confident of success. Rest assured, Natura, that more often than not your success is in the bag as long as you stay constant to your goal. A real assist for you is that latent within you is the primordial power of the goddess of nature, and she is as constant as the tides and the change of seasons. In fact, remembering the seasons is a good way for those born here to remember that nature is ruled by cycles. Accepting the fact that all of life ebbs and flows can keep Natura's children serenely, supremely confident. They can know at the deepest level of themselves that, as sure as day follows night, they will progress.

Looking at the other end of things, Natura's shadow side seems to emphasize its Saturn qualities over those of Jupiter. Driven and single-minded, Natura in the throes of its shadow becomes the classic type A personality, a self-centered, stubborn workaholic who is harsh to all who stand in the way. Another form that the shadow can take, however, is the opposite. Here Natura becomes apathetic, giving up on the very qualities that give this sign its great strength. Either way, Natura becomes morose and brooding, tending toward bitterness, self-isolation, loneliness, and depression. Both of these states effectively keep everyone who cares for you at bay, Natura, which only makes matters worse. You would be wise to let a little Jupiter in, seeing the light as well as the dark. A balance of mood is all-important for you to realize your highest ambitions. Never forget that Jupiter is expansion, while Saturn is contraction. You need both, in equal measure, to maintain stability and to function optimally.

No doubt the greatest goal for ambitious Natura is that of spiritual growth. The children of Natura are in a wonderful position to achieve just that. With the drive of one of the primordial god-forces powering them, they can make large strides in the spiritual arena. Sadly, all too often those born here relegate their spiritual side to the "I'll get to it later" pile. This is a huge mistake. With a developed spiritual side, Natura's children can reach even greater heights while being an inspiration to all those around them.

Relationships with someone born of Natura can be extremely challenging, if the Natura native is not sufficiently advanced. However, this takes time, and early marriages, for example, very often fail for those born here. Their natural intensity can lead to a strong sexual energy in them, and finding the right partner can be a frustration, as incompatibility is frequently a problem. Natura must make allowances for the personality of the other, and not try to rule or overwhelm in a relationship. The strong, introspective, determined part of Natura's make-up has a tendency to become so self-possessed that any other person is left out in the cold, emotionally speaking. Also, Natura in the grip of its shadow leaves no room for anyone else, putting any relationship at risk. However, when children of Natura can remain balanced, and pay attention to their spiritual growth while nurturing the relationship, an invincible pairing can result.

Natura is indeed fortunate when it comes to livelihood. The drive, determination, intensity, and confidence of this sign can bring satisfaction in a wide range of careers. Those of Natura are natural politicians as they can connect with others and gain their admiration and devotion with some ease. Their great focus makes them able to pursue research and other scientific positions. They are able to harness their abundant energy in the name of social causes, and their perseverance makes them great fighters for the oppressed. They can probe subjects deeply and with great insight, becoming go-to persons in any endeavor they attempt. Perhaps their greatest strength is their ability to be in any project for the long haul, if need be. A constant spirit like Natura's seldom leaves a career unsatisfied, or without leaving a lasting mark on the profession.

Concerning their health, balance is the key to Natura's emotional wellbeing. Moving too far in any direction for too long will have negative consequences for Natura. It is essential for those born here to modulate their emotions through practices such as meditation, yoga, and tai chi. A balanced, regular diet will help as well. Avoid extremes, Natura. Stomach problems can plague you, especially in later years. It's all about balance and moderation to help temper that intensity for which you are so justly famous. Spanning Sagittarius and Capricorn, Natura natives are also prone to the ills of those signs, including hip and thigh problems, difficulty with the bones and joints, and skin sensitivity. Regular exercise will be instrumental in assisting with musculoskeletal health, and Natura would be well-advised to keep such a program in place.

The symbol of this sign incorporates several elements. It combines a pyramid (for ancient religions, and concentration of power), whose sides suggest elephant tusks (for strength and Ganesha, the ancient Hindu god of good fortune), and the Sun, ruling planet of Natura. The animal associated with this sign is the mongoose. This animal is brave, more than willing to face the fearsome cobra. It is a symbol of protection, virtue, and devotion to a cause.

Natura, it takes some time to become acquainted with all the power at your disposal. Knowing how to handle your ability to persevere and achieve isn't something that is learned overnight. Yet, by taking your time and using those very qualities, you become the fulfillment of your potential. You are able to achieve virtually anything you truly desire. With balance and attention to your spiritual growth, you become almost invincible!

1804 – 1875 Natura, Jan 8 – Jan 20
1875 – 1946 Natura, Jan 9 – Jan 21
1946 – 2017 Natura, Jan 10 – Jan 22
2017 – 2088 Natura, Jan 11 – Jan 23
2088 – 2159 Natura, Jan 12 – Jan 24
2159 – 2230 Natura, Jan 13 – Jan 25

Apollo
January 23 – February 4
10.00 degrees Cap to 23.20

Animal – Monkey

Planet - Moon

Everybody has a path to follow, a life purpose. Yours, Apollo, is to help others find theirs. Sounds pretty straightforward, doesn't it? But you know how difficult it can be sometimes. So you continue to learn, understand, and research the human condition. Of course, you don't mind, because this is one of your favorite things to do. Philosophy, history, psychology, you name it. If its intent is to benefit humankind, you're all for it.

Like your namesake god, you like to reveal information. Apollo was the Greek god of prophesy, as well as healing, music, archery, and he was a protector of the young. As if that's not enough, he also later became associated with the Sun. In other words, Apollo was one busy god. He was a prime force in the punishment and destruction of the wicked; kind of a Judge Dredd of the Olympians (without the comic book persona). However, Apollo is usually associated with his finer side – music, poetry, and healing. As an overseer of prophets and oracles, such as the famous oracle at Delphi, he helped direct people to make the best decisions possible. Here's where the children of Apollo get that aspect of themselves, and the planetary energies of this sign help that along nicely.

This star is contained entirely within the astrological Sun sign of Capricorn, represented traditionally by a goat or a crocodile, and ruled by no-nonsense Saturn. Apollo itself is ruled by the Moon. This results in a curious mix of planetary goodies. The Moon brings a philosophical, exploratory piece, while Saturn serves to ground the energies and make them practical. This combination is very useful in helping Apollo's children work with others. Not only can you formulate the proper course of action as a counselor, for example, but you can also bring it through to the real world. Overarching these energies is the spirit of Apollo himself, a sun god, providing communication that is both clarifying and illuminating.

The natives of this star have some enviable gifts. They have a strong inner voice which keeps them focused. Their sense of principle is consistent and well developed, making them quite ethical and prone to uphold tradition, especially oral tradition. They are skilled speakers and writers, able to communicate clearly and in a way that allows easy understanding. They are seen by others as being intelligent and wise, and their opinion is sought out as a result. They are a kind and charitable lot as well. From all this comes a knack for the children of Apollo to be able to connect others with their best, natural path in life. They most often "hit the mark," as did Apollo, god of archery. In this regard, those born under this star help to dispel illusion and shine the light of truth upon others.

Apollo, you have been blessed (cursed?) with a restless mind. You constantly collect information, devouring subject after subject in an attempt to have whatever you need, whenever you need it. You're willing to travel the world to find the truth, too. Generally, you and your fellow Apollonians enjoy travel, especially when it results in more knowledge and a greater appreciation for humanity's many paths of endeavor. What's more, once you find the truth, you fervently seek to express it in your own life, and to share it with others. This is what makes you a great teacher, Apollo, in whatever field you pursue. It isn't all about telling, either. You are wise enough to know that much can be learned from listening to others; everyone is a potential teacher for you. Of course, your strong ability to listen makes you a better communicator, as you match wherever another is in terms of language and sophistication of expression. Everyone hears you talking their language, and this makes them even more trusting of you and interested in what you have to tell them.

Additionally, remember that Apollo is the god of performance-based endeavors, such as music. Interestingly, there is also an association of this sign with the Hindu goddess Saraswati, whose realm is learning and music. Many of Apollo's children can be found in musical fields for sure, but also in acting. You can be certain, however, that they will naturally take a traditional bent as their initial direction. For instance, Apollo, you will probably be attracted to being a classical musician; as a singer, opera may be your love; and as an actor, nothing compares with the stage.

Those born here must be careful of their shadow side, however. A love of tradition can become rigidity, with a definite, obstinate streak when it comes to change or embracing the new. Apollo, you must keep in mind that knowledge needs to evolve in order to remain vibrant. There is so much more to learn when you open yourself up to the force of change. Fortunately, this is a lesson that comes with time and most children of Apollo adjust as they age. Also, beware of becoming spiteful toward others. Most often, this urge arises in response to jealousy that you so frequently arouse in others. Your many gifts, as well as the fame and financial rewards that often flow from these gifts, can bring that jealousy about. There is a sensitive streak in your make-up that causes you to be easily hurt by the opinions of other people. In retribution, you may be tempted to engage in gossip, a fault that results from a warping of your natural communicative ability. Finally, some children of Apollo become so involved in studying and learning that they over-intellectualize everything, losing the heart of the matter, and with it the chance of true connection with anyone they try to help. Never forget your heart, Apollo. Your ruling planet, the Moon, is also a planet that connects closely with the kind, compassionate part of yourself. Feel the gift that the Moon gives you. Resist the pitfalls above, and you will advance along your spiritual path, while keeping your justly earned reputation.

Relationships with a child of Apollo can be very stimulating. There is always something new to talk about, and those born of Apollo aren't boring. It would be important, though, to find someone who shares your interests, or is at least willing to join you in your enthusiasm. You would not do well with someone who is uninterested in anything new. This would only open the rigidity of your shadow side, stifling your innate urges, and leading to dissatisfaction. You also would do best in a relationship where financial security is at least possible. You don't have to be involved with a multi-millionaire, just someone who isn't so free with cash that you are always living on the edge. There seems to be some anxiety about money in many born under Apollo, and the pursuit of financial comfort could wind up taking so much of your time that you short-change your inner drives toward knowledge and teaching others.

Some of the vocations that sit well with Apollo have already been mentioned, like teaching, music, acting, and counseling. Some other specific callings might include vocational coaching, speech therapy, or something in the travel industry. With the appeal of tradition, Apollo may also be very pleased to follow a path of traditional knowledge, such as astrology or religious studies. In short, any area that allows you to research, learn, and impart knowledge will keep you happy, Apollo. Never forget that you are an eternal student, so any field you enter should allow you to expand the knowledge therein. Vocational satisfaction will follow faithfully as a result.

In the realm of health, Apollo has its particular concerns. Problems with hearing or the ears are typical here, as well as sensitivity of the skin. Keep your ears protected from loud noises and be well aware of how you treat your skin. The Moon can bring concerns about the reproductive organs, while the Saturn influence can draw maladies of the knees or joint inflammation. This may bring about a change in gait, or an unusual way of walking, something to which this sign is prone.

Proper diet, hydration, and sufficient exercise can keep these risks at a minimum. Also, with such a busy mind, Apollo needs times of quiet and solitude. Make sure that you have some "alone time" on a regular basis to allow for peaceful study, reflection, and meditation. This will keep your stress level down, and your mind free so that it can absorb and organize even more learning.

The symbol for this sign resembles the crescent moon supporting the full moon. This implies listening to your inner wisdom, while attending to others. The three lines are the traditional "three uneven footsteps" of Apollo. These lines are connected to the rest of the symbol like lines of communication. The animal associated with this sign is the monkey, an animal of endless curiosity who is also very social, caring, and communicative.

You have a full plate of talents, Apollo. You observe, learn, investigate, and teach. You can fill the souls of others with your creative and counseling gifts. Helping others to help themselves. It's what you do. As long as you don't forget yourself in the process, you can become fulfilled, hitting your own target along the way.

1804 – 1875 Apollo, Jan 21 – Feb 2
1875 – 1946 Apollo, Jan 22 – Feb 3
1946 – 2017 Apollo, Jan 23 – Feb 4
2017 – 2088 Apollo, Jan 24 – Feb 5
2088 – 2159 Apollo, Jan 25 – Feb 6
2159 – 2230 Apollo, Jan 26 – Feb 7

Muses

February 5 – February 18
23.20 degrees Cap to 6.40 Aquarius

Animal – Lion

Planet - Mars

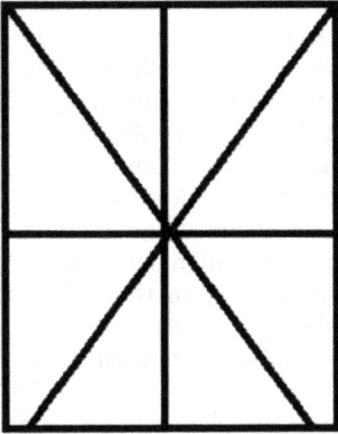

Are your favorite things singing, playing an instrument, dancing, or listening to music? Maybe it's spending your time composing songs, poetry, or works of fiction? If any of this rings true, you are in the groove of your special star. Those born here are the natural inspiration of the human race. Muses, you are able to move the emotions of those around you, uplifting their spirits or bringing them to tears. You help everyone to feel and experience.

Those fortunate enough to be born here have not one, but eight ruling deities. In mythology, the Muses were originally a group of nymphs that brought inspiration to people. Gradually, each took on a specific area of responsibility such as song, dance, poetry, comedy, or tragedy. By appealing to a particular muse, inspiration in that area could be granted. They were powerful sources of ideas and their practical execution. The astrological signs and planetary rulerships involved here fit perfectly with these traditional notions.

The Muses spans two astrological Sun signs, the latter part of Capricorn and the early part of Aquarius. Both of these signs are ruled by the practical planet Saturn, while Muses itself is ruled by energetic Mars. In fact, Mars is at the peak of its power in this sign. Astrologers call this position the exaltation of the planet, by the way. Mars in this sign plays the role of inspiration, just like the Tarot card called The Tower (associated with Mars) can represent "a bolt from the blue," shaking things up and causing a new way of looking at things. The double dose of Saturn in Muses, from Capricorn and Aquarius, gives its natives the ability to make it real, bringing the inspiration through to a finished product. After all, ideas are great, but unless they can be made manifest in physical reality, they are only flights of fancy – fun, but not particularly useful. The two Sun signs represented contribute mightily to the mix as well. Capricorn makes its way in the real world by manifesting and doing. Meanwhile, Aquarius holds sway in the realm of the mind, bringing ideas and a philosophical turn of thought.

Now, children of the Muses can really accumulate things, like material possessions or reputation. This is natural for someone with so much Saturn energy in their make-up. Sometimes, they can even become quite wealthy, either through inheritance or their own concerted effort. When they allow it, they can be bold and confident, thanks to that exalted Mars, though this is most often a trait that takes time to build. They usually possess a great ability for insight, and are excellent listeners, as the Muses operate through the senses. One of the primary quests of those born here is the search for truth, which can then be expressed through their creative works. Muses are commonly rather liberal in their thinking, and find themselves driven to take up a cause, uniting others to assist them in this regard. Muses, you could even be a leader, as others are captivated by your creative efforts and hold you in high regard.

A desire to travel comes naturally to those born under this star, and many find themselves spending part of their lives in foreign lands.

Think of it this way. Muses, you are in the lineage of the traveling, medieval minstrels. These creative, adventurous types would illuminate the minds of others, informing while entertaining. You carry on this grand tradition with your penchant for the arts. As a bonus, you may gain fame and fortune, increasing your influence even more.

But don't let all of this turn your head, Muses. You have a shadow side. In fact, if your head gets turned, this is when your shadow side comes roaring out. While in the grips of this negative energy, you can become greedy and self-absorbed. If this overly materialistic streak shows up, you will become stingy, miserly, grasping, and covetous. At its worst, narcissism sets in and the traveling minstrel becomes the self-possessed diva – aloof, arrogant, inconsiderate, ruthless, and vengeful. In other words, your Mars energy gets way out of control. You can avoid this with a proper dose of practical Saturn, cultivating patience and realizing that what you produce is a gift from the gods, rather than from your incredible, unassisted genius. In other words: You ain't all that.

Those born under the Muses also have a wonderful, inborn ability to achieve spiritual depth. After all, you are in close contact with the inspirational forces of heaven itself. Using your talents to bring the highest vibrations through, you can elevate yourself and all those who partake of your creations. Even if you use your connection with the divine to assist only yourself, through devotional songs or chants, for example, you raise the spiritual quality of anything else that you do. Such practices are always time and energy well spent, Muses. Don't allow these depths to go unplumbed.

Saturn's energy is a strong influence in relationships for those born here as well. Unfortunately, one of the areas ruled by Saturn is delay. Most often, this means that a child of the Muses will marry later in life, or will have a difficult time settling into a fine, long-term relationship for a goodly while. Even then, such unions can have more than their fair share of trouble and conflict. How to handle this? Well, with so much Saturn floating around, delay is basically par for the course. So don't panic, Muses, if you haven't found your true love before you turn thirty. In the long run, it's probably a blessing. Saturn's gift in the world of relationships is an improvement with age, so be patient. Looking at your prospective partner, someone you link with should be mature, able to handle your creative side, and not be threatened by any fame or notoriety you might achieve. In return, keep your inner diva well in check so that you don't come off as irrational or high strung (or high maintenance, for that matter). Instead, use your exalted Mars energy to add interest and excitement to the union.

It should come as no surprise that careers in music, art, dance, or writing can be very satisfying to a child of the Muses. Actually, vocational choices don't have to be limited to a strict interpretation of these areas. Anything that requires "artistry" for its execution can be a good fit, from mathematics to medicine. Also, due to Capricorn's influence, fields that require deft manipulation of the material world, like engineering or mining, even real estate or property management (thanks to Capricorn), will fulfill some Muses children. The force of Aquarius will pull some of those born here to charitable causes and philanthropic work. Many non-government organizations, for instance, would be very fertile ground for a child of the Muses to expend some energy. Those born under this star are often hard working and diligent, with a desire to explore their chosen area with vigor, awaiting the next bit of inspiration. As long as you can engage your creative side, Muses, a variety of vocations will bring you a sense of satisfaction and fulfillment.

As with all the signs, Muses have their own set of health-related concerns to be aware of. The exalted Mars energy of this sign can pre-dispose children of the Muses to trouble with blood pressure, heart difficulties, and problems with circulation in general, including hemorrhoids. It's all that Mars heat causing things to speed up or get stuck. The strong Saturn influence can bring joint and skeletal problems. It's as if Old Man Saturn ages the foundation of the body, the skeleton. Bony tissue is traditionally considered the densest and deepest of all the tissues of the body, while Saturn is the most grounding, dense planet in astrology. A match made in heaven, or rather on Earth. And in your bones. And your low back. Therefore, it is important for Muses to make sure that the body doesn't stay too stationary. Don't give Saturn a chance to make you rigid if you can help it. Move, Muses. After all, it's in your very soul to dance, to move, to make music. Using yoga or tai chi to provide a meditative aspect to the movement is a definite plus. For those so inclined, exalted Mars brings athletic prowess to this star. So if it matches your constitution and you have an interest, compete in sports. Most importantly, be sure to keep the joints adequately lubricated by drinking plenty of pure, fresh water. Keep your stress level, and your blood pressure, low with songs and chants, vibrating your being with the spirit of your guardian deities. You have a decided advantage over many other signs with the strong, natural affinity you have between your body and your spirit. Use it.

The symbol of this sign is a drum, crisscrossed with lines, making eight sections, to honor the eight muses and the music that is so much a part of this star. The animal associated with Muses is the female lion, a creature of great grace and quiet dignity. However, she can also be very bold and brash (Mars) when she needs to be. Knowing when to use that quality, however, takes time (Saturn) and is the great lesson of the finesse of this sign.

Muses, you are here to speak to the soul of humankind with your gifts. You show the rest of the world what it means to experience emotion for great benefit. You demonstrate the connection that exists between humanity and its source of inspiration. Share your wisdom and uplift us all!

1804 – 1875 Muses, Jan 3 – Feb 16
1875 – 1946 Muses, Jan 4 – Feb 17
1946 – 2017 Muses, Jan 5 – Feb 18
2017 – 2088 Muses, Jan 6 – Feb 19
2088 – 2159 Muses, Jan 7 – Feb 20
2159 – 2230 Muses, Jan 8 – Feb 21

Aegeon
February 19 - March 3
6.40 degrees Aquarius to 20.00

Animal – Horse

Planet - Rahu

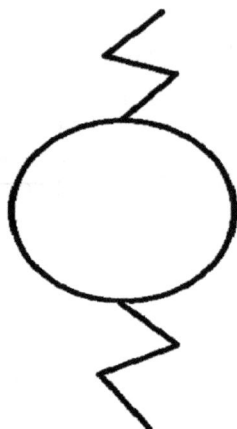

If you were born under this star, you know that you have a special purpose in this life. You may not be able to put it into words, but you have always known somehow. You understand deep within your being that you have been gifted with abilities that transcend the ordinary.

Those born under Aegeon intuitively know the depths. It comes naturally to them, and here's why. The name Aegeon comes from the mythological dwelling place of Neptune (Poseidon in Greek). This place was called Aegae, and it was deep under the sea. Neptune lived there with his horses and chariot. The horses of Neptune are not sea horses, but true horses with brazen hooves and golden manes. Neptune would ride along the surface of the water, drawn by these magnificent creatures. Given rulership of the seas when he drew lots with his brothers Zeus and Hades, Neptune was also given charge over earthquakes and tsunamis. He was the original mover and shaker.

Aegeon, you can tell what's going on, often at a level that defies verbal description. Neptune rules the water, which is a symbol for the unconscious and intuition. This is the area of consciousness where you feel most at home. Your intuition is quite strong and a guiding force for you. Sometimes this can be a problem, especially when you would rather not know what it tells you. Of course another way intuition can become a problem is if you ignore the lesson of the horse, the clever animal of this sign, refusing to use your intellect to filter intuitive messages. Blindly following flashes of intuition can lead to all sorts of trouble. Let the horses pull you through the seas, just as Neptune did.

Learning to shield yourself from unwanted or intense intuitive impressions is a necessary survival skill for you. If you cannot learn to work with this intense energy, you can fall victim to addictions or fantasy as ways of coping. These are very destructive paths for you, Aegeon, as they dull your natural talents and interfere with your ability to ground yourself in the present. Given your innate tendency to drift into otherworldy realms, anything that keeps you from being in the here-and-now is especially troublesome. In other words, you would be in danger of becoming an unfocused "space cadet." Fortunately, your sign is contained wholly within the astrological Sun sign of Aquarius, ruled by grounded Saturn, while Aegeon itself is ruled by Rahu, the North Node of the Moon. These planetary influences bring enough in-the-world energy that you can counter the Neptunian side of your soul. In fact, Rahu can bring not only psychic and intuitive skill, but the ability to turn that into earthly gain. Couple that with Saturn's natural manifesting ability, and you have a potentially winning combination.

Now, it can seem to others that you a bottomless well of understanding and healing, but you know better. Those of this star need to keep some parts of themselves private, and they require time and space for rejuvenation. It is too easy for you to shoulder the burdens of others, as a horse naturally does, forgetting your own needs. If you fall victim to this, you become vulnerable to picking up unwanted energies from those around you. Always remember that you can't help others if you are not taking proper care of yourself. You see the need around you, Aegeon, and seek to remedy it. However, this takes cautious application of your gifts, rather than pouring out an endless stream of them.

But take care, child of Neptune, when the depths call to you. For the depths can bring loneliness and depression, rather than the renewing solitude you crave at these times. After all, water is also a symbol for human emotion, and you readily experience the full range of them. This dark side of your nature can occur when Saturn and Rahu conspire to bring you down. When you are down, life can seem especially burdensome, and what was once a helpful healing stance can become an energy-sapping responsibility. This aids no one, least of all you. Connect rather with your inner strength (the positive sides of Saturn and Rahu), and recall your natural affinity for the empowering, mystical part of yourself.

Regarding opinions, Aegeons always have one; and they love to hold them tightly. This gives rise to the perception that you are stubborn and unyielding. When you are at your worst, Neptune's children, that view of you is absolutely correct. You can be so set that there's no talking to you. Perhaps this is why an Aegeon can have such difficulty in relationships. Stubborn and spacey (some might say aloof); what a tough combo to bring to a relationship! Therefore, openness (but not so open that your sensitive boundaries are overrun) is a necessary quality for you to cultivate. Give what you can; keep what you must – a good motto for all Aegeons.

Your generally quiet exterior can be shattered by the stress of too many demands. When caught off guard or too heavily burdened, you could find yourself pushed into a need to withdraw. At times like this, you can be very moody, and you will want to quote the Rolling Stones, "Hey! You! Get off of my cloud!" Resist this temptation to engage in extreme drama, however, as it only serves to alienate others. You can see now why relationships are often a challenge, can't you, Aegeon?

Your sun sign of Aquarius the water-bearer aligns you with new and revolutionary ways of thinking and being. Leading humanity in new directions is a primary mission for Aquarians, and healing from a spiritual orientation is Aegeon's part of that mission. You can do this as both a practitioner and as a role model. For example, the Aegeons are naturally attracted to the healing arts. But they might also find themselves in the position of a teacher, a religious leader, or an astrologer. While the responsibility of these vocations can feel overwhelming, those of Aegeon birth are also blessed with innate knowing and certainty. These talents allow you to show courage in the face of frustration and daunting tasks. You are usually very certain of your opinion and the rightness of your course.

Regarding health, proper self-care is a must. You often do not have the rooted, rugged reserve of some of the other stars. Meditation is especially helpful for you, as it grounds you while clearing the energetic debris you may have picked up from others. Movement practices such as yoga and tai chi will lend a helping hand, nourishing your energy as well as your spirit. Mineral or aromatherapy baths can also help release any unwanted energy that you may have accumulated along the way. Certainly, proper diet is a key ingredient as well. Be sure to include grounding foods such as root vegetables in your choices.

The symbol for your sign is an empty circle with lightning bolts emanating from it. This is emblematic of the subtle force present in everything, a force that you can appreciate with your innate connection to the subtle energies. The bolts are also like electrons, emphasizing this concept. Taken as one, the symbol can seem like a turtle, the carrier of the world in some creation accounts (and you truly can identify with this when feeling especially burdened). The turtle, though, can also plumb the depths of the sea, while being at home on land. That is your purpose, Aegeon – to bring the gifts of the deep, mystical parts of humanity to common realization in everyday existence. The horse is the animal given to this sign. Associated with healing ability, the horse also brings the power of the intellect and the ability to see to the root of a problem. Aegeons certainly are healers, but they approach healing from a metaphysical, philosophical perspective. They heal from the level of spirit.

You present a challenge to many, children of Aegeon, as others can find it difficult to fathom your depths. Try not to be too harsh at those times. Remember, you are here to show the way toward a fuller expression of the mystical and spiritual dimensions. This is a hard road for many to understand. Your patience will reward you and those you are in contact with.

Your special contribution is essential in order for humanity to evolve. Neptune, god of the sea and earthquakes; Aegeon, bringer of mystical insight that shakes the establishment and causes outmoded structures to crumble. An important mission, and one that you were born to fulfill!

1804 – 1875 Aegeon, Feb 17 – Mar 1
1875 – 1946 Aegeon, Feb 18 – Mar 2
1946 – 2017 Aegeon, Feb 19 – Mar 3
2017 – 2088 Aegeon, Feb 20 – Mar 4
2088 – 2159 Aegeon, Feb 21 – Mar 5
2159 – 2230 Aegeon, Feb 22 – Mar 6

Chimera
March 4 - March 16
20.00 degrees Aquarius to 3.20 Pisces

Animal – Lion

Planet - Jupiter

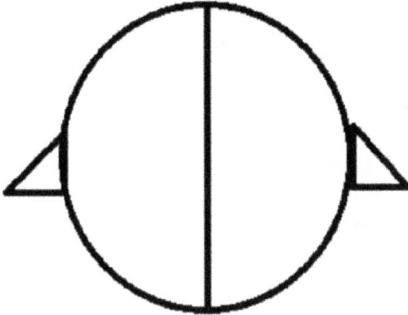

Some people were born to make a difference in this world. These are the people who see what needs changing and go about doing just that. You, Chimera, are one of those people. You might be seen as a rebel or an eccentric, but what does that matter? You see your duty, and you do it. Some might say that such actions take courage, but to you it's simply what needs to happen. It's not your fault that others can't see it as well as you do.

The Chimera of ancient myth was a fire-breathing beast, most popularly shown as a creature made of three parts, a lion, a goat, and a dragon. In some accounts, Chimera also had three heads, one for each animal that made up its body. Whenever it appeared, it was an omen of storms or other disasters. Additionally, Chimera was associated with a volcano in Lycia, now a part of Turkey. People took strong notice whenever Chimera put in an appearance, since things were never boring when this creature was around (obviously). This is also the case concerning those born under this star. People cannot ignore the children of Chimera, because they might just pay the price if they do.

This particular star spans two astrological Sun signs, Aquarius and Pisces. Aquarius is ruled by Saturn, while Pisces is ruled by Jupiter. Chimera itself is also ruled by Jupiter. The energies here give a combination of expansiveness, with an undercurrent of contraction. What does all this mean? Well, those born here can be quite idealistic, with grand ideas and a strong identification with causes and social issues (Jupiter-like energy). They would also like to see solutions to these problems put forth and enacted (practical, Saturn-like tendencies). Chimerans can be rather in-your-face about it (with all that Jupiter), and difficult when frustrated (Saturn can brood, sometimes getting pretty dark in the process). The children of Chimera can be volatile shakers, like the quakes and spewing lava that come with a volcanic eruption. Their ideas can be revolutionary, and those born here are often very original in their thinking. Just as lava leads to the formation of new soil, the ideas of Chimera can bring forth fertile ground for new approaches to old problems.

One of the main features shared by those born of Chimera is a continuous striving for greater accomplishment and improvement, both in themselves and in those around them. There is a strong, almost aggressive streak in them that respects no obstacle. They see it as their duty to make things happen. This often takes the form of self-improvement, or suggestions (maybe orders?) that those around them grow as well. Chimera, you can talk a good game, and you can be quite convincing in your presentation. Often, others are at a loss when it comes to countering your approach. You are opinionated, of that there is no doubt; and you're not shy about sharing your views of things. Your intelligence shines through your arguments, and your focus is strong. That is why sometimes you are described as over-powering, insistent, even pushy. Now, you may not see yourself that way, but that isn't necessarily the perception of others. You have lots of Jupiter energy. That makes for expansive, even grandiose, ideas and interventions. The sky's the limit, they say, but you might not appear to believe even that. Always reaching, always aspiring, that's you in a nutshell. Ultimate satisfaction, unfortunately, often eludes you.

So here is something to watch out for, child of Chimera. You have a striving nature. Nothing is too big to tackle. In your mind, anyway. The practicality of your dreams and schemes, though, may tell a different story. Of course, you are often successful. You are clever and resourceful. You have powerful ideals and you have the drive to see them through. Nevertheless, you can reach too far, too fast. Taken by your own process, you might find yourself engaging in risky behavior, sometimes with frustrating or unintended consequences. When met with frustration or disappointment, your darkness can arise. What might this look like?

A frustrated Chimera can brood and complain. Loudly. At times like these, no past glory holds any satisfaction. All that you may have accomplished in the past seems lacking, simply not enough. Everything is empty. You may hear people tell you that you are never satisfied, that you are too restless, or that you can't see the good that you have accomplished. Your response to these statements may be cynical, and it's quite possible that you will feel boxed in, stymied at every turn; and this can lead to depression or anxiety. But look carefully, Chimera. Be sure that it wasn't you that did the boxing in. For instance, you may have alienated an important someone in the realization of your plans. You may have over-reached (all that Jupiter, remember) and not waited for the proper moment to act. You know how tough it is to take the counsel of others, especially when you have your sights set on something; but that is exactly what you might need to do. Another area to look at when you are feeling dark is the tendency to over-achieve, so common in this sign. Sometimes this can mask a fear of death, as if you are running as fast as you can to escape it. Word of advice: You aren't going to escape it. Nobody does. Calm and center yourself. Become comfortable with the transience of all things. Put yourself in the Now, not in the what-I've-done past or the what-I-still-gotta-do future.

Your dark side has other features, too. Beware of selfishness, anxiety, impulsivity, and explosive anger. You can also get pretty loud, as if that will make your position more convincing. These unattractive features of your personality can show their faces whenever you are unable to balance the expansive, Jupiter force with the contractive, Saturn force. Whenever you find yourself like this (and don't worry; if you don't see it, someone will make it apparent to you either directly or by avoiding you entirely), it's your cue to go inward. This can be tricky territory for you, Chimera, but increasing your connection to your spiritual core will bring the balance you so sorely need at times like these. Take some time for yourself. A bit of seclusion can facilitate your process.

Possibly nowhere else does the challenge to find balance arise so prominently for Chimera than in the area of relationships. In this arena of life, it's all too common a tale to have those of this star find a relationship, only to have it fizzle, sometimes spectacularly so. Chimera, you have a strong need for relationship, almost a desperation, but that can work against you. For instance, you can be quite opinionated, which may certainly lead to conflict. Add to that the tendency you have to look at things from several directions (remember those three heads of Chimera?), and you can look inconsistent, even insincere or dishonest. There can be times when your approach will serve to sabotage an otherwise good relationship. It's no wonder that you may get the reputation for being tough to be with. When a relationship is under stress, you are certainly not at your best. Under these circumstances, your Saturn energy will move to "circle the wagons," giving the impression that you are uninvolved or self-absorbed. In order to counter this, you must be able to show vulnerability and open yourself to the views of the other. That can be difficult, to be sure. You're not really used to doing that – not all that often, anyway. But this is the growing edge that you need to cultivate in order to avoid a series of bad relationships. If a relationship is going badly, ask yourself if there is anything you are doing to sabotage it; and be honest. You could even (gasp!) ask the other about this possibility. Listen carefully to what is offered. Keep your defensiveness in check. If needed, go inward and seek answers there. You may be surprised at what you find. Any Chimera that can successfully navigate the waters of relationships is a goodly ways down the road of personal growth.

In the world of vocations, a child of Chimera can flourish in any area that needs new eyes and fresh approaches. Areas of research, business leadership, or helping professions that encourage innovation and an individualized approach are all fertile places for Chimera to look for job satisfaction. Those of a more eccentric bent can even consider off-beat areas such as the occult sciences for their niche. With their quick minds and original thoughts, the places for Chimera to find fulfillment in work are many.

Health concerns for the children of Chimera come from the Sun signs it encompasses, and the planetary energies involved. Piscean influences can bring foot and ankle trouble, as well as a tendency toward addiction (alcohol, drugs, food, sex, etc.). This then brings trouble to the liver. All the intensity that you possess can result in stress-related illnesses such as ulcers, heart, and circulatory system concerns. Also, be aware of problems in your legs due to the Aquarian part of your nature. To counter this, take care when you exercise, making sure that you warm up well beforehand. Don't overdo, either, you alway-striving, gotta-do-more Chimeran, you. Moderation is the key, and it will counter any tendency toward addiction. Finally, make a connection with your spiritual side. Meditation and quiet reflection will calm the stressful tendency of your nature.

The symbol for Chimera reflects the complexity of this sign. It is like a profile of someone with two faces, indicating both the multi-faceted personality of its natives, and the transition from life to death. The sharpness of the features, like a sword, symbolizes the take-no-prisoners attitude and quick mind of Chimera, and the occult symbolism of the sword with the element of Air, of which Aquarius is the fixed sign. The animal associated with Chimera is the male lion, an animal of courage whose roar is not to be ignored. You certainly can seem like that when you have an idea or opinion that needs to be heard. But a male lion also does not have to humble himself or beg, reminding you to keep your dignity when expressing yourself.

Chimera, you are a beacon for new ideas and novel approaches. If you can keep your tendency to be overpowering in its place, you can bring humanity to an evolved place, filled with the noblest of sentiments and

the worthiest of causes. Use your abilities sagely, and the world will be
a better place for your being in it.

1804 – 1875 Chimera, Mar 2 – Mar 14
1875 – 1946 Chimera, Mar 3 – Mar 15
1946 – 2017 Chimera, Mar 4 – Mar 16
2017 – 2088 Chimera, Mar 5 – Mar 17
2088 – 2159 Chimera, Mar 6 – Mar 18
2159 – 2230 Chimera, Mar 7 – Mar 19

Phorcus
March 17 - March 30
3.20 degrees Pisces to 16.40

Animal – Bull

Planet - Saturn

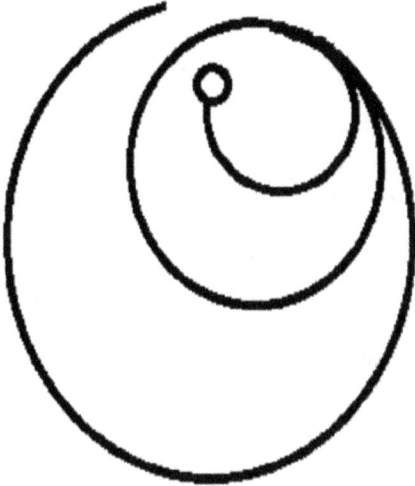

Every family needs someone like you. You're the person who is always willing to give and to share, and you stick up mightily for those you love. Often, you know what people need before they do. You are simply that in tune with those close to you.

In mythology, Phorcus was an ancient sea god who ruled the deepest parts of the ocean, including the strange and wonderful creatures that inhabit those depths. Phorcus with his wife Ceto gave birth to many of the fantastic sea monsters of ancient lore as well. As such, seafarers propitiated Phorcus, seeking his favor and asking for his protection during perilous voyages. Phorcus ruled over the most mysterious places on the planet, and had the respect and awe of any who ventured near his realm. The planetary energies involved with this star reflect these mythological themes.

Phorcus is contained entirely within the astrological Sun sign of Pisces, the fish. So, the association with the depths of the sea is a given. Pisces is ruled by Jupiter, while the sign of Phorcus itself is ruled by Saturn. This combination of planets yields a mixture of expanding and contracting energies. Saturn is often equated with the depths, while Jupiter reveals the heights. The expanded awareness credited to Pisces in the form of intuition or psychic ability comes from the Jupiter influence. Phorcus, ruling the depths, harkens forth the Saturn energies. This means that the children of Phorcus are psychically sensitive without being too "air-headed." There is a practical sense about them, while they also possess the sympathetic, kind-hearted tendencies of a true Piscean.

Those born of Phorcus are rather generous as a rule, giving of themselves to those in need, especially those close to them. They are charitable to the point of being overly self-sacrificing, sometimes to their detriment. As a result, Phorcus, you need down time. Serious down time. Solitude is very important to you, so that you can re-charge. Giving all the time is a guaranteed way to burn out, so having some time just for yourself isn't a luxury. It is an absolute necessity. If you don't have such time built into your life now, make sure you start to do so, and fast. Without it, you'll tire and you won't be of any good to anyone. Perhaps you've noticed that already?

When you take proper care of your need for solitude, Phorcus, you can be quite cheerful, and give gladly. Without that base, however, giving can become a chore. Even though you are driven to give, you can become resentful and angry if it feels like too much of an obligation. Hobbies and distractions are a must, to allow you to rest in things that bring you simple joy. Writing has traditionally been a rewarding pastime for those of this star, but in modern times, photography has become a very popular way of expressing that inner, creative drive. Photography means "writing with light," and many children of Phorcus take this route to express themselves. Travel, either in fact or in mind, is another common pursuit for Phorcus. Imagine being a travel photographer for a charitable organization! Talk about an ideal situation . . .

You have high ideals, Phorcus, and you are willing to devote energy to seeing them through. Though you aren't necessarily at the forefront, making the headlines, you are there, giving all you can for whoever you feel needs care and support. You are more of a foot soldier than a general, but as we all know, it's the foot soldiers that actually get the job done.

A central goal for anyone born under this star is spiritual development. Children of Phorcus have a strong intuitive gift, which they can handily use to plumb the depths of the unconscious. It is absolutely essential that they use this gift for their own growth in the spiritual realm. It is part of their mission. In order to feel truly at ease in this world, those of Phorcus must dip into the depths, their natural habitat. A primary tool for accomplishing this goal is meditation. This practice is so important that children of Phorcus are not fulfilling their destiny without it. A meditation practice can become part of the time of seclusion that is so important for the well-being of any Phorcus. Concentrated success here will ultimately deepen the intuitive gift that Phorcus has, assisting in even greater spiritual development and energy to help others.

Neglecting these core needs will make it easier for the shadow side of Phorcus to emerge from the deep. When in the grip of this shadow, Phorcus manifests many of the qualities of negative Saturn energy. Secrecy, cunning, anger (usually expressed passive-aggressively), laziness, and irresponsibility are often seen at these times. Phorcus, you are not likely to become overtly aggressive, since your Saturn energy lends some self-control. However, while in the grip of the shadow, emotions can vary from high to low to anywhere in between, sometimes changing pretty rapidly. You can even become obsessively focused on an enemy, real or imagined, when you get like this. It then becomes the aim of your existence to defeat or best that enemy, and it is a tremendous waste of your potential. Guard against this at all costs.

Another sign of your dark side is a tendency toward addictions (to alcohol, drugs, sex, food, sugar, etc.). This is in evidence when you are not attending to your core needs for solitude and spiritual development. Addiction then becomes the anesthetic or insulation from a painful or depleting life. Be extremely careful here. Notice any danger signs and seek to short-circuit them as soon as possible, for they can be very damaging for you and those close to you.

Speaking of those close to you, relationships are often a challenge for those born here. Despite your caring, giving nature (thanks to Jupiter), the road to relationship happiness is often a rough one (there goes that negative Saturn again). Perhaps it is precisely because you are so giving. Kind, generous, caring individuals often attract those who would take advantage of those very qualities, either consciously or unconsciously. Co-dependence is a common problem in your relationships, Phorcus. You give so much that the other can become extremely comfortable in the role of taker. You will know when this is happening. You will feel worn out, while taking less time for yourself. You may feel that excessive demands are being placed upon you, and resentment will begin to make itself known. At times like these, be sure to stop and listen to your inner senses, as they are very strong and reliable in you.

All this is not to say that Phorcus is incapable of a rewarding, mutually nourishing relationship. Certainly this is possible. But it comes only when you are balanced within yourself, keeping the energies of Jupiter and Saturn stable and cooperating. When you feel supported as well as supportive, you are definitely on the right track.

In the world of work, the natural, giving bent of Phorcus fits well with charitable and non-profit organizations. That yen for travel can bring those born here satisfaction in any part of the travel industry. As mentioned before, writing and photography also appeal naturally to those of this star. Using their intuitive gifts, some areas of occult science, like astrology or psychic reading, may be attractive. With their interest in ideas, many children of Phorcus have found satisfaction in teaching, or in religious or philosophical fields. Basically, any career in which a Phorcus can give, share, and make the world a better place for those in need makes for a good fit.

The health challenges for Phorcus center around the energies of the planets involved in its makeup, as well as the kind and open nature of this sign. Foot and leg problems come from the Piscean energy, coupled with Jupiter and Saturn influences. Having a sensitive nature, easily influenced by the environment around them, digestive and bowel problems can occur, along with allergies of various sorts. Another way this may manifest can be in hypertension or other stress-related disorders. If Phorcus falls victim to addiction, areas such as the liver may be affected. To counter these trends, care should be taken with diet and the intake of any potentially addictive substances. Moderation is the key for anyone trying to balance the push-pull of the Jupiter-Saturn dynamic. Gentle exercise can also be useful in maintaining internal balance and managing stress. Pay close attention to keeping the immune system healthy in order to protect against stress-related illnesses and allergies. Finally, the underpinning of all this is a strong basis in meditation and nourishing solitude.

The symbol for this sign reflects the natural affinity for, and the strong need to connect with, the depths. Phorcus is depicted here as a serpentine figure descending in waves down into the unconscious, where the pure source of the life force dwells. The animal associated with this sign is the bull, a sturdy, solid, dependable creature, a repository of strong, inner strength, capable of shouldering many burdens in service to others.

Phorcus, you have the unique gift of being able to travel to the depths, bringing back wisdom that can benefit all of humanity. Your selfless, giving nature benefits those to whom you lend your service. In solitude, you grow in strength, so that you may return and assist those in need. You blend inner wisdom and outer service, a formidable combination for change and growth!

1804 – 1875 Phorcus, Mar 15 – Mar 28
1875 – 1946 Phorcus, Mar 16 – Mar 29
1946 – 2017 Phorcus, Mar 17 – Mar 30
2017 – 2088 Phorcus, Mar 18 – Mar 31
2088 – 2159 Phorcus, Mar 19 – April 1
2159 – 2230 Phorcus, Mar 20 – April 2

Hermaia
March 31 – April 12
16.40 degrees Pisces to 30.00

Animal – Elephant

Planet - Mercury

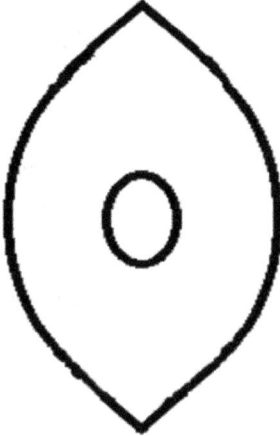

You're an easy person to talk with. Surely you've been told that more than a few times. It seems that people are attracted to your nourishing, supportive energy. Not only that, but others come to you for advice on any number of topics. You simply seem to understand, and you usually know what to say, too – or at least you know where to point people so that they get what they need.

It's no surprise that you are able to talk with pretty much anyone about pretty much anything. This star is ruled by Hermes (Mercury to the Romans), god of communication, travel, commerce, and social interaction. Very busy god, that Hermes. He had many areas of responsibility. Traveling quickly from place to place, Hermes even served as the messenger for the other gods and goddesses. The Hermaia was actually a festival held in honor of Hermes, complete with athletic contests. The astrological associations of this star, as well as the personality characteristics of those born here, clearly flow from this mythology.

Hermaia is the final star in the cycle of the 27 stars of Asterian astrology. It is contained wholly within the astrological Sun sign of Pisces the fish. This Sun sign is ruled by Jupiter, while Hermaia itself is ruled by Mercury. That combination of planetary energies gives a generally expansive personality that exudes an easy confidence, and someone who is very comfortable talking. On fact, those born under this star can talk a blue streak, and often about almost anything. There is a strong athletic interest in this star too, especially in men born here. Yet, these guys don't come off as stereotypically macho. The reason for this is that Venus is exalted, as astrologers say, in this star. This means that Venus's finest qualities are fully in evidence here. The push of Venus energy brings a very nurturing, supportive touch to Hermaia, making those born here real softies, in the best possible meaning of the term. Compassion resides in the deep core of Hermaia's children.

Hermaia, you love to take care of others, and are extremely generous to those you feel closest to. You are always ready to extend a helping hand, lend money, or become a strong support to those in need. You typically feel right at home shouldering some extra responsibility, knowing that it is making life a little easier for someone else. These qualities flow from your very essence. It's almost as if you have absorbed the lessons of the other 26 stars, and so are able to blend those lessons for the greater good of humanity.

Unlike others born in the Sun sign of Pisces, those of Hermaia tend to have less trouble with the addictions that can often trouble Pisceans. Nor are the children of Hermaia prone to the ungroundedness that can frequently mark a Piscean temperament. They have been blessed with the ability to bring the best qualities of Pisces to the material plane. They are the true nurturers of the zodiac.

Being born under Hermaia gives someone a leg up in the quest for spiritual growth, too. They are searchers after the greatest truths of existence, and seem to soak up spiritual wisdom like a sponge.

Between this ability and the many acts of kindness that they perform, the children of this star can build up quite a bit of positive karma in this life.

Hermaians have an intuitive understanding of the higher planes of existence, even though they may not appear that way on the surface. All that most people know about them is that they are nice, caring individuals who often have a way with animals. While males born here are frequently gifted, or are at least quite interested, in sports, females tend to be gifted in the arts. The daughters of Hermaia are able to bring forth creations from the depths of their intuition. In all those born here, the intuitive gift contributes to their inherent sense of support and nourishment of others. They just seem to know what is going on with another person, which makes it easier to meet the needs of those they assist.

Sounds ideal, doesn't it? Not exactly. It's not a perfect existence being born under this star. Your natural supportive streak can be used against you, Hermaia. You have probably had the experience of someone wanting to get close to you simply to use what you have to offer. Often, this is an unconscious process. The other just knows that you are really helpful and caring. But be careful about how you spread your caring around. You have a strong capacity to carry the burdens of others. However, there are those who will wish to hitch a ride on your largesse, and give nothing in return. Remember that sometimes being supportive requires demanding an equal partnership. Give, but watch out for over-giving. You aren't helping anyone who wishes merely to take advantage of you.

Like all stars, Hermaia has its dark side. As one might expect, this expresses as the opposite of your best qualities. In the grip of your negative side, you can be selfish, vengeful, and stubborn. Being a giving person, you can feel unappreciated and slighted by others, which can result in sulking or lashing out in anger. Look for this to happen especially in relationships where you are giving so much and getting so little in return. At your best, you are not covetous or petty.

At your worst, however, you are grasping and looking for the slightest insult to becomes enraged about.

In relationships, though, Hermaia can be quite a catch. In fact, the men of Hermaia are traditionally considered to make the best husbands – loving, giving, attentive, protective, etc. In other words, an all-around good guy. And the women are no slouches either. They are kind and giving, devoted and supportive. All this comes with a caveat for the children of Hermaia, however. It is too easy for them to have their helping nature used against them by those who would take advantage of them. As a result, many born under this star can have a difficult time in relationships. You need to use your internal barometer, Hermaia, in order to weed out the users from the genuinely good partners. If you begin to feel slighted or used up in a relationship, it's time to take a second look. Someone as giving as you deserves a partner that appreciates those wonderful qualities of yours, and is willing to give back. Remember that the nurturer needs nurturing too.

In the world of career, Hermaia can find satisfaction in a number of areas. Service industries may appeal to that natural need to nurture and take care of others. For example, humanitarian organizations are a natural fit for a child of Hermaia. Even careers involving restaurants, hotels, or other places of food, lodging, and comfort can work out very well. Religious vocations are another fruitful arena, especially in those orders and groups that perform humanitarian work. Since the children of Hermaia love to enlighten others toward a higher path, writing and teaching in areas that support that aim are promising. Politics appeals to some Hermaians, as this path is seen as a way to benefit a large number of people. Finally, careers in the travel industry draw some of the children of this star. After all, Hermaia as Hermes is a traveler. Many of this star travel in spirit, while others find fulfillment in the physical manifestation of this urge. Regardless, any career that appeals to Hermaia's natural proclivities toward giving and nurturing will feel rewarding.

Health concerns for Hermaia stem mainly from its rulership by Mercury, and its being wholly contained within the Sun sign of Pisces.

As with all Pisceans, foot and ankle problems can occur with Hermaia. Therefore, concern with proper footwear is essential. While not plagued to the extent of others born under Pisces, addictions can be a pitfall, especially abuse of alcohol. Moderation is the key. In other words, don't "drink like a fish." Since Mercury also rules youth, there is a possibility that those of this star struggled more with illness as a child than many of their peers. Mercury brings sensitive digestion and a touchy nervous system to those it rules as well. Hermaia may have problems, therefore, with indigestion and nervous tension. Additionally, sleep difficulties may arise from the high energy of Mercury. Nightmares can occur from Hermaia's highly developed intuition being too open to outside energetic influences. For all these concerns, respites from the world of giving to others is important. Periods of seclusion and a regular meditation practice will help here. Finally, spend some time near water. The rhythm of the domain of Pisces will be soothing to the Hermaian soul.

The symbol for Hermaia suggests both the stylized image of the fish of Pisces and the eye of compassion, which sees the suffering of the world while seeking to remedy it. The eye also calls to mind the wisdom that comes from a life of good karma as that life draws to a close. The animal associated with this star is the elephant, a creature seen as being able to carry many and heavy burdens – but always with kindness, patience, and unfailing willingness. Conversely, the elephant is an animal famous for its stubbornness, a trait that allows Hermaia to bear up under responsibility, but a trait which can also become inflamed by its darker traits.

Hermaia, you culminate the cycle of the 27 stars. In you resides the wisdom and compassion gathered by experience and intuitive knowing. You can be a visionary. You can lead the world, or at least those who know and love you, into a brighter, fuller future!

1804 – 1875 Hermaia, Mar 29 – April 10
1875 – 1946 Hermaia, Mar 30 – April 11
1946 – 2017 Hermaia, Mar 31 – April 12
2017 – 2088 Hermaia, April 1 – April 13
2088 – 2159 Hermaia, April 2 – April 14
2159 – 2230 Hermaia, April 3 – April 15

Asterian Astrology and the 12 Sun signs

The 27 signs of Asterian astrology overlay and modify the traditional Sun signs of astrology. For example, there are three distinct types of Aries: a Dioscuri Aries, a Hades Aries, and a Vesta Aries. As a result, the Asterian signs and the traditional Sun signs interact and influence each other. Much has already been written about the traditional signs in a multitude of astrology books. Therefore, they will be covered only in brief here, for the purpose of a quick reference.

Aries

April 13 – May 14

Aries is the first sign of the zodiac. It is a Fire sign and is ruled by Mars. Its symbol is the ram. Those born here tend to be independent with a strong "let's do it" force in their personality. They are creative and are great at starting new projects. They can be quite competitive and dynamic in their presentation. As a result, Aries often gravitates toward sports, the military, or any executive position. Nevertheless, they tend not to be overly physically aggressive, preferring to fight with words and ideas. They bounce back from disappointments and nothing seems to be able to keep an Aries down for long. Always ready to start again, those born in Aries like to lead, and often do a good job when in positions of authority. They can be willful, impulsive, and headstrong; however, at their core they are largely compassionate and loving, which can make them effective healers. Their plans and schemes are usually meant to benefit others, even when they don't seem like that on the surface. Often, tact is an acquired taste for an Aries. Those born here can come off as opinionated and critical, but this approach is most often employed with the improvement of others in mind. They can best progress spiritually when they use their minds and energy in the search for ultimate truth.

1804 – 1875 Aries, April 11 – May 12
1875 – 1946 Aries, April 12 – May 13
1946 – 2017 Aries, April 13 – May 14
2017 – 2088 Aries, April 14 – May 15
2088 – 2159 Aries, April 15 – May 16
2159 – 2230 Aries, April 16 – May 17

Taurus
May 15 – June 13

Taurus is the second sign of the zodiac. It is an Earth sign and is ruled by Venus. Its symbol is the bull. People born here tend to be stable, shrewd, reliable, and fixed in their ways of doing things. They have an innate appreciation for beauty in all its forms, and love orderly surroundings. For example, their homes tend to be well appointed and comfortable. Additionally, Taureans have a tendency to accumulate and hold onto things, such as money, property, or weight. Liking material comfort, those born under Taurus enjoy the finer things of life. They are devoted in relationships, sometimes remaining in a situation that is no longer satisfying, due to their bullish constancy. At their worst, they can be quite stubborn. They are slow to anger, but once aroused, can be cruel, even vicious. However, they can most often be counted on to be reliable friends, steadfast and loyal. Just don't get on their bad side, as they don't mind carrying a grudge around – for a long time. They can be opinionated and will remain fixed in their ways of thinking and doing things until they come to feel the need for a change. They enjoy working with their hands, and prefer to leave a lasting impression on the physical plane. In spiritual matters, those born under Taurus prefer traditional, ritualistic approaches to devotion.

1804 – 1875 Taurus, May 12 – June 11
1875 – 1946 Taurus, May 13 – June 12
1946 – 2017 Taurus, May 15 – June 13
2017 – 2088 Taurus, May 16 – June 14
2088 – 2159 Taurus, May 17 – June 15
2159 – 2230 Taurus, May 18 – June 16

Gemini
June 14 – July 14

Gemini is the third sign of the zodiac. It is an Air sign and is ruled by Mercury. Its symbol is the twins, or a couple. Those born of Gemini tend to be personable and generally kind. They are almost never malicious, and often retain their youthful looks. Geminis are interested in ideas and innovation, and love to explore using their sharp minds. They, however, can over-extend themselves and become anxious and agitated, even neurotic. They are the natural communicators of the zodiac, and many become writers and entertainers. They love working with information, and can often be found in the scientific and computer fields as well. Geminis like to stay active, and they remain on the go, either physically or mentally, until they exhaust themselves. It is a major challenge for those born here to learn to regulate their energy. When turned in the wrong direction, their natural way with communication can lead to an unreliable, dishonest individual. However, even in these cases they are mostly interested in getting what they can, versus intentionally injuring others. Another downfall is Gemini's potential to be indecisive and not bring plans to fruition. In spiritual matters, though, if they are able to turn their nimble minds in a higher direction, they can find peace and calm.

1804 – 1875 Gemini, June 12 – July 12
1875 – 1946 Gemini, June 13 – July 13
1946 – 2017 Gemini, June 14 – July 14
2017 – 2088 Gemini, June 15 – July 15
2088 – 2159 Gemini, June 16 – July 16
2159 – 2230 Gemini, June 17 – July 17

Cancer
July 15 – Aug 15

Cancer is the fourth sign of the zodiac. It is a Water sign and is ruled by the Moon. Its symbol is the crab. People born here are generally friendly and nurturing. They care deeply about those close to them, and are invested in having a good home life. In fact, Cancers are very protective and can lash out at those seen as a threat to their domestic peace. They follow their emotions in most matters, making them naturally responsive to the feeling tone of individuals, groups, and society as a whole. Cancer loves big ideas and can embark on large projects with great excitement. When they become fixated, however, their viewpoint can narrow to the point of ineffectiveness. Their ability to feel deeply can make them quite contemplative and considerate, but if they draw inward too much, surly defensiveness can assert itself. When confident, Cancers easily influence and lead others. This is because their natural affinity for sensing a situation's emotion gives them an edge in their dealings with others. They can become rather devoted to anything into which they invest their emotions. They will then stick with it until they become completely disillusioned, and turn their investment elsewhere. When Cancers open themselves up to receiving the energy of spiritual truth, their compassionate bent can be used to the great advantage of everyone.

1804 – 1875 Cancer, July 13 – Aug 13
1875 – 1946 Cancer, July 14 – Aug 14
1946 – 2017 Cancer, July 15 – Aug 15
2017 – 2088 Cancer, July 16 – Aug 16
2088 – 2159 Cancer, July 17 – Aug 17
2159 – 2230 Cancer, July 18 – Aug 18

Leo

Aug 16 – Sept 15

Leo is the fifth sign of the zodiac. It is a Fire sign and is ruled by the Sun. Its symbol is the lion. Leos like order, and will do whatever is needed to bring that about. They have a strong sense of self and feel best when they are in the lead or the center of action. They feel most comfortable when dominant and react strongly to anything they see as threatening their autonomy. Leos can be rather dramatic in their presentation, seeming larger than life. They are generally intelligent and usually possess fine verbal skills. Taken to extremes, though, their natural tendencies can result in vanity and arrogance. Those born here can have trouble allowing anyone close to them to think and act for themselves, as Leos prefer to call all the shots. On the positive side, they can inspire others to great heights with their caring support. Leos can become effective healers through the strength and force of their personality, and their drive to get things done. They set high standards for themselves, which can become a burden if not handled wisely. This can lead to feelings of failure, a big pitfall for a Leo. Their greatest challenge is in learning to channel their authority and dominant energies properly. Doing so brings them a central calm that allows for much spiritual growth and advancement.

1804 – 1875 Leo, Aug 14 – Sept 13
1875 – 1946 Leo, Aug 15 – Sept 14
1946 – 2017 Leo, Aug 16 – Sept 15
2017 – 2088 Leo, Aug 17 – Sept 16
2088 – 2159 Leo, Aug 18 – Sept 17
2159 – 2230 Leo, Aug 19 – Sept 18

Virgo
Sept 16 – Oct 15

Virgo is the sixth sign of the zodiac. It is an Earth sign and is ruled by Mercury. Its symbol is a virgin or a young girl. Those born under this sign possess good, quick minds, fine verbal skills, and a nervous temperament. Virgos have good memories and are a storehouse of facts. As such, they are great providers of information, which they can use to their advantage. They have a natural pre-occupation with health and wellness. This is because Virgos tend to have delicate constitutions, especially regarding digestion. They can easily fall prey to chronic illnesses, made worse by their mental focus on whatever ails them. Nevertheless, Virgos can excel at the healing arts when they focus their mental energies appropriately. Their appreciation for detail makes them competent artists and craftsmen. Those born here must watch their tendency to overwork, especially when it springs from feeling that they aren't being recognized for their contribution to a cause. They can overtax their energies if they do not keep a fine awareness of them. When they turn their demanding inner nature outward, they can seem fussy and hard to please. But if the can put their discerning minds toward spiritual matters, especially areas devoted to fine, philosophical determination, they will be rewarded with inner peace.

1804 – 1875 Virgo, Sept 14 – Oct 13
1875 – 1946 Virgo, Sept 15 – Oct 14
1946 – 2017 Virgo, Sept 16 – Oct 15
2017 – 2088 Virgo, Sept 17 – Oct 16
2088 – 2159 Virgo, Sept 18 – Oct 17
2159 – 2230 Virgo, Sept 19 – Oct 18

Libra
Oct 16 – Nov 15

Libra is the seventh sign of the zodiac. It is an Air sign and is ruled by Venus. Its symbol is the scales or balance. Those born under this sign are creative, and can have grand designs for humanity. They are visionaries and idealists, often with the sense of bringing transcendent beauty to the world. However, Libras can feel that the way to harmony is through disharmony, and can sometimes appear dark in their approach. They have little trouble expressing sexuality, and can use their charisma to influence others. With their love of beauty, they can gravitate toward the arts or theatre, all for the betterment of humankind. Libra's drive for harmony, coupled with their social orientation can also attract them to the political life. Libras love influence and enjoy being the catalyst for change in those around them. Taking their talents to excess, they can become agents for leading themselves and others down a destructive path. Libras must maintain awareness of their natural abilities and use them for betterment of others. Truly, it is common for Libras to make their mark in the world in whatever endeavor they focus upon. They have an ability to connect with higher states of consciousness. Therefore, putting their energy toward connecting with spirit can move Libras rapidly along the path of development.

1804 – 1875 Libra, Oct 14 – Nov 13
1875 – 1946 Libra, Oct 15 – Nov 14
1946 – 2017 Libra, Oct 16 – Nov 15
2017 – 2088 Libra, Oct 17 – Nov 16
2088 – 2159 Libra, Oct 18 – Nov 17
2159 – 2230 Libra, Oct 19 – Nov 18

Scorpio
Nov 16 – Dec 14

Scorpio is the eighth sign of the zodiac. It is a Water sign and is ruled by Mars (and Pluto in Western astrology). Its symbol is the scorpion. Those born here like to explore the depths of anything they contact. Their Mars rulership gives them an affinity for physical expression and skill in martial endeavors. Yet, they can also devote themselves to matters of the mind, becoming talented researchers or therapists. Scorpios can easily become focused on the uses of energy, either external or internal, and techniques for these uses are often a fascination for them. They are quite perceptive as a rule, and form their views accordingly. Scorpios are not particularly flashy and may be underestimated as a result. Those born here can be difficult for others to figure out, as they keep their emotions a bit closer to the vest than the other Water signs. As such, they often appear mysterious or cautious. When their talents are improperly utilized, a Scorpio can become ensnared in the dark side of life. However, the proper channeling of their strengths leads to a deep, spiritually connected individual, someone in tune with their subconscious as well as their higher self. Using this connection, a Scorpio can reach great levels of true insight and a deep communion with the realm of spirit.

1804 – 1875 Scorpio, Nov 14 – Dec 13
1875 – 1946 Scorpio, Nov 15 – Dec 14
1946 – 2017 Scorpio, Nov 16 – Dec 15
2017 – 2088 Scorpio, Nov 17 – Dec 16
2088 – 2159 Scorpio, Nov 18 – Dec 17
2159 – 2230 Scorpio, Nov 19 – Dec 18

Sagittarius
Dec 15 – Jan 12

Sagittarius is the ninth sign of the zodiac. It is a Fire sign and is ruled by Jupiter. Its symbol is the centaur or archer. Those born here tend to have a positive outlook on life. While they have a strong sense of law, justice and "what is right," they are also very optimistic and altruistic. The friendly manner of Sagittarians makes them good companions, and they are interested in the betterment of the whole. They like their space, and enjoy moving about. This love of movement is true in Sagittarian thinking as well, though they tend to stay on the conventional side of things. Lovers of the outdoors, they gravitate toward time in nature. They are philosophical and love to think, forming strong opinions, though this can become a problem if they take themselves too seriously. Nevertheless, they enjoy a good time, and can be rather social. Always ready to lend a helping hand, Sagittarians are an asset to almost any enterprise. Their expansive nature makes them a joy to be around most of the time, and life tends to bring them luck. But those born here aren't all about good times and book learning. Sagittarius has a decidedly spiritual side. They tend to approach even this from a philosophical perspective, but often have high hopes and justified expectations of spiritual attainment.

1804 – 1875 Sag, Dec 13 – Jan 10
1875 – 1946 Sag, Dec 14 – Jan 11
1946 – 2017 Sag, Dec 15 – Jan 12
2017 – 2088 Sag, Dec 16 – Jan 13
2088 – 2159 Sag, Dec 17 – Jan 14
2159 – 2230 Sag, Dec 18 – Jan 15

Capricorn
Jan 13 – Feb 11

Capricorn is the tenth sign of the zodiac. It is an Earth sign and is ruled by Saturn. Its symbol is the goat or the crocodile. In many ways the most practical of the signs, Capricorn is often concerned with the material world. Those born here are hard-working, patient, and willing to play the long game. They value most those things that come to them through their own hard work. Often ambitious, they usually set lofty goals for themselves, and are willing to work long and hard to attain them. Capricorns are the businessmen of the zodiac, with clever and shrewd minds. They can be very mechanical as well, often excelling in the hard sciences and research. Paradoxically, Capricorns can also be rather humorous in their approach to life. Those born under this sign can experience obstacles in the attainment of their stated ends, but use these setbacks as a foundation for even higher attainment. Capricorns are not easily dissuaded from the marks that they set for themselves. This obstinacy can make them difficult to deal with, especially if they perceive the aims of others as being in conflict with their own. When mired in the material world, their spiritual growth is stunted. It is important, therefore, for Capricorns to learn to avoid workaholism, looking beyond the material to the spiritual underpinnings of the world.

1804 – 1875 Cap, Jan 11 – Feb 09
1875 – 1946 Cap, Jan 12 – Feb 10
1946 – 2017 Cap, Jan 13 – Feb 11
2017 – 2088 Cap, Jan 14 – Feb 12
2088 – 2159 Cap, Jan 15 – Feb 13
2159 – 2230 Cap, Jan 16 – Feb 14

Aquarius
Feb 12 – March 13

Aquarius is the eleventh sign of the zodiac. It is an Air sign and is ruled by Saturn (and Uranus in Western astrology). Its symbol is the water bearer. At their highest, those born here are free thinkers and innovators. Aquarians possess incisive minds, perceive clearly what needs to be done, and can invent the future. At their worst, they are self-critical, doubting of their abilities, feeling blocked, and confused. An evolved Aquarian is devoted to the good of humanity, even sacrificing their own needs for the collective. They are the champions of the oppressed. Unevolved Aquarians may find themselves degraded, while uncomplainingly accepting a repressed position in the world. Aquarians can rise to the greatest heights, or sink to the greatest depths. In any case, they are often seen as eccentric – either as original thinkers or as oddballs. Those born here are inherently spiritual, however, and can do well if they devote themselves to a spiritual path. Aquarians possess an ability to transcend the ego for their own greater development. In leadership positions, they can take their followers along a most exalted path by their inspiration. The major challenge for Aquarians is to use their ability to connect with spirit to uplift the rest of humanity. If their minds remain clear and they connect with their innovative tendencies, Aquarians can achieve much success in the spiritual realm.

1804 – 1875 Aquarius, Feb 10 – Mar 11
1875 – 1946 Aquarius, Feb 11 – Mar 12
1946 – 2017 Aquarius, Feb 12 – Mar 13
2017 – 2088 Aquarius, Feb 13 – Mar 14
2088 – 2159 Aquarius, Feb 14 – Mar 15
2159 – 2230 Aquarius, Feb 15 – Mar 16

Pisces

Mar 14 – Apr 12

Pisces is the twelfth sign of the zodiac. It is a Water sign and is ruled by Jupiter (and Neptune in Western astrology). Its symbol is the fish. Those born here are very emotional by nature. They are in touch with their intuitive and psychic sides, and often make decisions based on "gut feelings." Their emotional tendency can make Pisceans quite impressionable and vulnerable to the influences of others. They may also drift in imagination, becoming ungrounded. However, they are seen generally as very kind individuals who go with the flow. Those born here have a highly developed sense of compassion, though this can be used against them by the unscrupulous. Things which impact the emotions, such as music and the arts, can bring a Piscean great joy. They love the sensations of the body, and cultivating grace. They can even become good athletes. Pisceans may dwell on negative emotions, however, which can lead to various types of addiction and other forms of self-undoing. Their strong involvement with emotion can lead to disturbances in that realm, as well as bringing self-doubt and over-identification with feelings. This can make them inconstant and impractical. It is the greatest challenge of Pisces to attain control over emotion and channel their considerable intuitive gifts toward greater realizations of the spirit.

1804 – 1875 Pisces, Mar 12 – Apr 10
1875 – 1946 Pisces, Mar 13 – Apr 11
1946 – 2017 Pisces, Mar 14 – Apr 12
2017 – 2088 Pisces, Mar 15 – Apr 13
2088 – 2159 Pisces, Mar 16 – Apr 14
2159 – 2230 Pisces, Mar 17 – Apr 15

Rahu and Ketu (Head and Body of Medusa)

The Medusa was an ugly creature. Let's have a look at how she came into existence, for she wasn't always that ugly... Again, the Gods played their role.

The Medusa was the daughter of Phorcus and Ceto, the children of Gaea (Earth) and Oceanus (Ocean). She was one of the three sisters known as the Gorgons. The other two sisters were Sthenno and Euryale. Medusa was the only mortal out of the three. She was originally a golden-haired and very beautiful maiden, who, as a priestess of Athena, was devoted to a life of celibacy; but, being wooed by Poseidon, whom she loved in return, she forgot her vows, and became united to him in marriage. For this offence she was punished by the goddess in a most terrible manner. Each wavy lock of the beautiful hair which had so charmed her husband, was changed into a venomous snake; her once gentle, love-inspiring eyes now became blood-shot, furious orbs, which excited fear and disgust in the mind of the beholder; whilst her former roseate hue and milk-white skin assumed a loathsome, greenish tinge.

Seeing herself thus transformed into so repulsive an object, Medusa fled from her home, never to return. Wandering about, abhorred, dreaded, and shunned by all the world, she now developed into a character worthy of her outward appearance. In her despair, she fled to Africa, where, as she passed restlessly from place to place, infant snakes dropped from her hair, and thus, according to the belief of the ancients, that country became the hotbed of these venomous reptiles. With the curse of Athena upon her, she turned into stone whomsoever she gazed upon, till at last, after a life of nameless misery, deliverance came to her in the shape of death, at the hands of Perseus who decapitated her. Her head became **Rahu** the North Node and created Solar Eclipses, and her body became **Ketu** the South Node and created Lunar Eclipses.

These two planets in Asterian astrology do not appear in the common Western system but are known in India as Rahu and Ketu (the Hindu story of Rahu is very similar to the Greek story of Medusa), which are the North and South nodes of the Moon, respectively. These planets are always located exactly opposite each other in a person's astrology chart. Medusa's head and body are not actual, physical planets, but rather points in the sky where the Moon's orbit intersects the ecliptic (the apparent path of the Sun in the sky). The nodes are also where eclipses occur. Even though Medusa's head and body are considered "shadow planets," they can be potent forces in a person's chart or personality. Since they are unfamiliar to many people in the West, they are briefly described below.

Medusa's Head, Rahu

Rahu (Medusa's Head) is the North (ascending) node of the Moon. It is also known as the dragon's head (caput draconis in Latin). This planet is an expansive force, but of a generally negative sort. It can disrupt a person's energy and carry a person away with societal trends, as if hypnotized by a culture. Being expansive, Rahu's greatest effects are in the outer world. When under the influence of Rahu, a person is more likely to develop neuroses or neurological disorders – in short, any abnormal sensitivity of the mind. Rahu also influences criminality, and can give rise to strange diseases, problems with drug abuse, and paranoia. But not all is bad with Rahu. This planet can also give material power, popularity, prestige, and wealth. Yet, while it can be quite fulfilling outwardly, it can leave a person inwardly wanting. A strong Rahu personality is marked by narcissism, charisma, easy power over others, and an overestimation of self. It is a very active energy, leading to overstimulation, greed, and lawlessness.

Medusa's Body, Ketu

Ketu (Medusa's Body) is the South (descending) node of the Moon. It is also known as the dragon's tail (cauda draconis in Latin). This planet is contractive in nature and is also negative, but generally less so than Rahu. While under its influence, Ketu can grant a person great powers of concentration and mastery of arcane subjects. However, Ketu brings self-doubt and a desire for isolation, as well as a lowering of self-confidence and a decreased sense of self-worth. There is also a tendency to over-accommodate to others and become strongly self-sacrificing. At times, however, these feelings are overcompensated for by a drive toward megalomania and extreme cruelty. In its dealings, Ketu tends to bring sudden change, for good or ill. Under its spell, a person can accumulate a great deal of wisdom, especially about the occult or even psychic powers; but it can just as easily bring profound confusion. A Ketu personality is gifted spiritually, but plagued by insecurity and an underestimation of self. Such people also have a strong interest in the occult and the afterlife.

As you can see, these two shadow planets can be quite influential. Usually, the exact nature of their influence is determined by their position relative to other planets in the chart. Yet, there are those whose entire personality is influenced by a strongly placed node, even more so if their Asterian sign is ruled by Rahu or Ketu.

Axial Precession

also known as Precession of the Equinoxes

by Jade Luna

Now, for those of you who want the technical explanation for all this Eastern versus Western reckoning of the zodiac, read on. If you are spooked by scientific jargon, or don't care about the details, feel free to skip this part, even though it is pretty interesting.

In astronomy, **axial precession** is a gravity-induced, slow and continuous change in the orientation of an astronomical body's rotational axis. In particular, it refers to the gradual shift in the orientation of Earth's axis of rotation, which, like a wobbling top, traces out a pair of cones joined at their apexes in a cycle of approximately 26,000 years (This is called a Great or Platonic Year in astrology). The term "precession" typically refers only to this largest, secular motion; other changes in the alignment of Earth's axis — nutation and polar motion — are much smaller in magnitude.

Earth's axial precession was historically called **precession of the equinoxes** because the equinoxes moved westward along the ecliptic relative to the fixed stars, opposite to the motion of the Sun along the ecliptic. As a result, the Sun appears to move slowly backwards through the constellations, year by year. The term "precession of the equinoxes" is still used in non-technical discussions, in other words, when detailed mathematics is absent. Historically, Hipparchus is credited with discovering precession of the equinoxes. The exact dates of his life are not known, but astronomical observations attributed to him by Ptolemy date from 147 BC to 127 BC.

With improvements in the ability to calculate the gravitational force between planets, during the first half of the 19th century, it was recognized that the ecliptic itself moved slightly. This was named **planetary precession** as early as 1863, while the dominant component was named **lunisolar axial precession**. The combination of these was named **general axial precession,** instead of precession of the equinoxes. Lunisolar axial precession is caused by the gravitational forces of the Moon and Sun on Earth's equatorial bulge, causing Earth's axis to move with respect to inertial space. Planetary axial precession (actually an advance) is due to the small angle between the gravitational force of the other planets on the Earth and its orbital plane (the ecliptic), causing the plane of the ecliptic to shift slightly relative to inertial space. Lunisolar axial precession is about 500 times larger than planetary precession. In addition to the Moon and Sun, the other planets also cause a small movement of Earth's axis in inertial space, making the contrast in the terms "lunisolar" versus "planetary" misleading. As a result, in 2006, the International Astronomical Union recommended that the dominant component be renamed the **precession of the equator** and the minor component be renamed **precession of the ecliptic**, but their combination is still named general precession.

The axial precession of the Earth has a number of observable effects. First, the positions of the south and north celestial poles appear to move in circles against the space-fixed backdrop of stars, completing one circuit in 25,772 Julian years (given the approximate rate of change in 2000). Thus, while today the star Polaris lies approximately at the north celestial pole, this will change over time, and other stars will become the "north star." The south celestial pole currently lacks a bright star to mark its position, but over time axial precession will also cause bright stars to become "south stars." As the celestial poles shift, there is a corresponding gradual shift in the apparent orientation of the whole star field, as viewed from a particular position on Earth.

Second, the position of the Earth in its orbit around the Sun at the solstices, equinoxes, or other time defined relative to the seasons, slowly changes. For example, suppose that the Earth's orbital position is marked at the summer solstice, when the Earth's axial tilt is pointing directly towards the Sun. One full orbit later, when the Sun has returned to the same apparent position relative to the background stars, the Earth's axial tilt would not now be tilted directly towards the Sun. Due to the effects of axial precession, the tilt is a little way "beyond" this. In other words, the solstice occurred a little earlier in the orbit. Thus, the tropical year, measuring the cycle of seasons (for example, the time from solstice to solstice, or equinox to equinox), is about 20 minutes shorter than the sidereal year, which is measured by the Sun's apparent position relative to the stars. Note that 20 minutes per year is approximately equivalent to one year's shift per 25,772 years, so after one full cycle of 25,772 years, the positions of the seasons relative to the Earth's orbit are "back where they started." (In actuality, other effects also slowly change the shape and orientation of the Earth's orbit, and these, in combination with precession, create various cycles of differing periods; for example, Milankovitch cycles. The magnitude of the Earth's tilt, as opposed to merely its orientation, also changes slowly over time, but this effect is not attributed directly to axial precession.)

For identical reasons, the apparent position of the Sun relative to the backdrop of the stars at some seasonally fixed time, say the vernal equinox, slowly regresses a full 360° through all twelve traditional constellations of the zodiac, at the rate of about 50.3 seconds of arc per year (approximately 360 degrees divided by 25,772), or 1 degree every 71.6 years.

Hipparchus and Ptolemy

Though there is still-controversial evidence that Aristarchus of Samos possessed distinct values for the sidereal and tropical years as early as c. 280 BC, the discovery of precession is usually attributed to Hipparchus of Rhodes or Nicaea (190–120 BC), a Greek astronomer. According to Ptolemy's *Almagest*, Hipparchus measured the longitude of Spica and other bright stars. Comparing his measurements with data from his predecessors, Timocharis (320–260 BC) and Aristillus (~280 BC), he concluded that Spica had moved 2° relative to the autumnal equinox. He also compared the lengths of the tropical year (the time it takes the Sun to return to an equinox) and the sidereal year (the time it takes the Sun to return to the same position relative to a fixed star), and found a slight discrepancy. Hipparchus concluded that the equinoxes were moving ("precessing") through the zodiac, and that the rate of precession was not less than 1°

in a century, in other words completing a full cycle in no more than 36,000 years.

Virtually all of Hipparchus's writings are lost, including his work on precession. They are mentioned by Ptolemy, who explained precession as the rotation of the celestial sphere around a motionless Earth. It is reasonable to assume that Hipparchus, like Ptolemy, thought of precession in geocentric terms, as a motion of the heavens.

Hipparchus gave an account of his discovery in *On the Displacement of the Solsticial and Equinoctial Points* (described in *Almagest* III.1 and VII.2). He measured the ecliptic longitude of the star Spica during lunar eclipses and found that it was about 6° west of the autumnal equinox. By comparing his own measurements with those of Timocharis of Alexandria (a contemporary of Euclid who worked with Aristillus early in the 3rd century BC), he found that Spica's longitude had decreased by about 2° in about 150 years. He also noticed this motion in other stars. He speculated that only the stars near the zodiac shifted over time. Ptolemy called this his "first hypothesis" (*Almagest* VII.1), but did not report any later hypotheses Hipparchus might have devised. Hipparchus apparently limited his speculations because he had only a few older observations, which were not very reliable.

Why did Hipparchus need a lunar eclipse to measure the position of a star? The equinoctial points are not marked in the sky, so he needed the Moon as a reference point. Hipparchus had already developed a way to calculate the longitude of the Sun at any moment. A lunar eclipse happens during the full moon, when the Moon and the Sun are in opposition. At the midpoint of the eclipse, the Moon is precisely 180° from the Sun. Hipparchus is thought to have measured the longitudinal arc separating Spica from the Moon. To this value, he added the calculated longitude of the Sun, plus 180° for the longitude of the Moon. He did the same procedure with Timocharis's data (Evans 1998, p. 251). Observations like these eclipses, incidentally, are the main source of data about when Hipparchus worked, since other biographical information about him is minimal. The lunar eclipses he observed, for instance, took place on April 21, 146 BC, and March 21, 135 BC (Toomer 1984, p. 135 n. 14).

Hipparchus also studied precession in *On the Length of the Year*. Two kinds of year are relevant to understanding his work. The tropical year is the length of time that the Sun, as viewed from the Earth, takes to return to the same position along the ecliptic (its path among the stars on the celestial sphere). The sidereal year is the length of time that the Sun takes to return to the same position with respect to the stars of the celestial sphere. Precession causes the stars to change their longitude slightly each year, so the sidereal year is longer than the tropical year. Using observations of the equinoxes and solstices, Hipparchus found that the length of the tropical year was 365+1/4–1/300 days, or 365.24667 days (Evans 1998, p. 209). Comparing this with the length of the sidereal year, he calculated that the rate of precession was not less than 1° in a century. From this information, it is possible to calculate that his value for the sidereal year was 365+1/4+1/144 days (Toomer 1978, p. 218). By giving a minimum rate, he may have been allowing for errors in observation.

To approximate his tropical year, Hipparchus created his own lunisolar calendar by modifying those of Meton and Callippus in *On Intercalary Months and Days* (now lost), as described by Ptolemy in the *Almagest* III.1 (Toomer 1984, p. 139). The Babylonian calendar used a cycle of 235 lunar months per 19 years since 499 BC (with only three exceptions before 380 BC), but it did not use a specified number of days. The Metonic cycle (432 BC) assigned 6,940 days to these 19 years producing an average year of 365+1/4+1/76 or 365.26316 days. The Callippic cycle (330 BC) dropped one day from four Metonic cycles (76 years) for an average year of 365+1/4 or 365.25 days. Hipparchus dropped one more day from four Callipic cycles (304 years), creating the Hipparchic cycle with an average year of 365+1/4–1/304 or 365.24671 days, which was close to his tropical year of 365+1/4–1/300 or 365.24667 days. The three Greek cycles were never used to regulate any civil calendar—they only appear in the *Almagest* in an astronomical context.

We find Hipparchus's mathematical signatures in the Antikythera Mechanism, an ancient astronomical computer of the 2nd century BC. The mechanism is based on the following combination of cycles: the solar year; the Metonic Cycle, which is the length of time it takes the Moon to reappear in the same star in the sky with the same phase (full Moon appears at the same position in the sky approximately every 19 years); the Callipic cycle (which is four Metonic cycles and more accurate); the Saros cycle; and the Exeligmos cycles (three Saros cycles for accurate eclipse prediction). The study of the Antikythera Mechanism proves that the ancients used very accurate calendars based on all the aspects of solar and lunar motion in the sky. In fact, the Lunar Mechanism, which is part of the Antikythera Mechanism, depicts the motion of the Moon and its phase, for a given time, using a train of four gears with a pin and slot device. This apparatus gives a variable lunar velocity that is very close to the second law of Kepler, i.e. it takes into account the fast motion of the Moon at perigee and its slower motion at apogee. This discovery proves that Hipparchus's mathematics was much more advanced than Ptolemy describes in his books, as it is evident that Hipparchus developed a good approximation of Kepler's second law.

The first astronomer known to have continued Hipparchus's work on precession was Ptolemy in the 2nd century. Ptolemy measured the longitudes of Regulus, Spica, and other bright stars with a variation of Hipparchus's lunar method that did not require eclipses. Before sunset, Ptolemy measured the longitudinal arc separating the Moon from the Sun. Then, after sunset, he measured the arc from the Moon to the star. He used Hipparchus's model to calculate the Sun's longitude, and made corrections for the Moon's motion and its parallax (Evans 1998, pp. 251–255). Ptolemy compared his own observations with those made by Hipparchus, Menelaus of Alexandria, Timocharis, and Agrippa. He found that between Hipparchus's time and his own (about 265 years), the stars had moved 2°40', or 1° in 100 years (36" per year; the rate accepted today is about 50" per year or 1° in 72 years). Ptolemy also confirmed that precession affected all fixed stars, not just those near the ecliptic, and his cycle had same period of 36,000 years, as found by Hipparchus.

Michael J. Santangelo, Ph.D.

Michael J. Santangelo has been a student of the esoteric and the occult since his teen years. This interest led him to pursue a career in psychology, in which he holds a doctorate. Even after his formal academic studies concluded, however, Santangelo strove to enrich his practice by incorporating a variety of "alternative" approaches into his work with others. He has training in Asian bodywork, Chinese herbalism, various forms of energy work (including two lineages of Reiki, quantum healing, and medical intuition), and attained a second doctoral degree in Traditional Naturopathy. Additionally, he is a graduate of the 16-year program of study offered by Builders of the Adytum, a Western mystery school of the highest caliber. He uses all of these approaches in his therapeutic work.

Santangelo includes disciplines such as astrology, numerology, and Tarot in his professional work as well, finding these to be valuable adjuncts to his other skills. He has been a teacher, both formal and informal, most of his life. Santangelo has taught classes at all levels, from community education to graduate school. Additionally, he and his wife operated a massage school for ten years, in which he did much of the teaching. Aside from co-authoring this book, Santangelo has published in the areas of psychology, massage therapy, and Tarot. He has served as editor of the Tarot section of the website of All Things Healing. He is the author of *Nine Miles To Freedom: The paths of the human psyche* and the forthcoming *Essential Virtues of the Major Arcana: A new look at the roadmap of the soul*. He maintains a private practice in Iowa City, Iowa, and can be reached via his website www.ninemilestofreedom.com

Jade Sol Luna

Jade S. Luna is the mind behind the reconstruction of the oldest Astrology book "The Yavanajataka" into Asterian Astrology. He became certified in Astrology from the A.F.A in Arizona, D.A. in India and the A.I.V.S in Santa Fe, New Mexico. Luna has written for several magazines including Hinduism Today and Luna has been featured on several radio shows across the world.

Jade Luna has traveled extensively around the planet, (India 34 times, Thailand 7 times and Europe 10 times) lecturing and conducting workshops on Astrology and Ancient Roman-Greco mysticism. Jade has spent a great deal of time with various teachers, Saints and Sadhu's in Asia and around the globe.

Jade Luna consults with people privately. He usually presents a few seminars each year at various locations world wide.

During and after Luna's formal Astrological training, Bhau Kalchuri (disciple of Meher Baba) and Kal Babaji (Khajuraho India), tutored him in advanced mysticism and other forms of classical Indian lore. Jade Luna has now transformed his Indian studies into a Greco-Roman practice, showing the spiritual connection that the Ancient Mediterranean had with India.

Jade Luna is the author of Asterian Astrology, Hecate: Death, Transition and Spiritual Mastery and Hecate II: The Awakening of Hydra. Jade has been one of the most successful Astrologers in the world and has maintained a high level practice for over 19 years. www.jadesolluna.com

Glossary

*Asterian Astrology symbols by Bobbie James

What is a Star?

In the Asterian Astrology and Vedic (Hindu) system of Astrology, known in Sanskrit as Jyotish, the 27 constellations and not the 12 star-signs are the key to understanding celestial influences on our planet. These 27 constellations are known as the 27 Stars or the Nakshatra, which are 300 to 400 light years away from earth. Based on a person's Star at the time of birth, Asterian offers a more powerful predictive technique compared to other forms of astrology.

Precession of the Equinox (simple)

In astronomy, **axial precession** is a gravity-induced, slow, and continuous change in the orientation of an astronomical body's rotational axis. In particular, it refers to the gradual shift in the orientation of Earth's axis of rotation, which, similar to a wobbling top, traces out a pair of cones joined at their apices in a cycle of approximately 26,000 years (called a Great or Platonic Year in astrology).

The Yavanajataka, (The core philosophy of Asterian Astrology)

The **Yavanajātaka** (Sanskrit: *yavana* 'Greek' + *jātaka* 'nativity' = 'nativity according to the Greeks') of **Sphujidhvaja** is an ancient text in Indian astrology.

It is a later versification of an earlier translation into Sanskrit of a Greek text, thought to have been written around 120 BCE in Alexandria,[1] on horoscopy. The original translation, made in 149–150 CE by "Yavanesvara" ("Lord of the Greeks") under the rule of the Western Kshatrapa king **Rudrakarman** I, is lost. Only a substantial portion of the versification 120 years later by Sphujidhvaja under Rudrasena II has survived.

Yavanajataka is the earliest known Sanskrit work dedicated to horoscopy. It was followed by other works of Western origin which greatly influenced Indian astrology: the Paulisa Siddhanta ("Doctrine of Paul"), and the Romaka Siddhanta ("Doctrine of the Romans"). **Jade Sol Luna** reconstructed the Yavanajataka and recreated the book to fit the modern age of Astrology, and this system is called Asterian Astrology.

Jade Sol Luna INC Publishing

Copyright.JadeLuna@AsterianAstrology
www.asterianastrology.com